# Guerrilla Warfare in the Corporate Jungle

# Guerrilla Warfare in the Corporate Jungle

*Adaptations for Survival*

by

K.F. Dochartaigh

**BEP**

BUSINESS EXPERT PRESS

*Leader in applied, concise business books*

*Guerrilla Warfare in the Corporate Jungle: Adaptations for Survival*
Copyright © Business Expert Press, LLC, 2021.

First published in 2021 by
Business Expert Press, LLC
222 East 46th Street, New York, NY 10017
www.businessexpertpress.com

ISBN-13: 978-1-95253-884-1 (paperback)
ISBN-13: 978-1-95253-885-8 (e-book)

Business Expert Press Business Law and Corporate Risk Management Collection

Collection ISSN: 2333-6722 (print)
Collection ISSN: 2333-6730 (electronic)

Cover and interior design by S4Carlisle Publishing Services Private Ltd., Chennai, India

First edition: 2021

10 9 8 7 6 5 4 3 2 1

Printed in the United States of America.

*For Ava—Audentes Fortuna Iuvat*

# Description

This book is a survival manual for life in the corporate world which guides the reader on how best to navigate it's pitfalls and avoid being trapped. It fuses three separate but intertwined disciplines of the Animal kingdom, The Guerrilla battlefield and the corporate world to help establish patterns of behaviour and understand the motivations that underpin each action.

All three areas share a common environment; the jungle, where visibility is limited and ambush is the only method of attack by predators. The book blends animal and human psychology and gives safe passage in all its encounters.

The book has been meticulously researched with animal behaviours documented and applied to the study of human psychology with additional research on Military techniques and combat psychology on ambush and counter insurgency also included in the attempt to understand and react to conflict in the workplace.

This book is designed to assist people at any stage in their career to better understand the motivations that underpin human interactions within the workplace. I have attempted to fuse three separate but closely related environments to highlight patterns and similarities that we can use to better ourselves in our daily interactions in our working lives.

As stated above; the corporate world, the animal kingdom and the battlefield all seem like an unlikely amalgamation but you will see that that all environments share common objectives, strategies and interdependencies that underpin everyday survival.

This book does not condone war, quite the opposite as you will see it takes more of a defensive position in repelling attacks and seeks to promote the occurrence of collaboration over individual competition which will also become apparent. It is not a 'call to arms' or a promotion of anarchy, not by any stretch of the imagination, as it merely assists the individual in adapting within their environment in order to ensure their survival. Whether you work as an Accountant, IT consultant, Lawyer, Salesperson or Project Manager; the same logic still applies as there is a natural order in all corporate vocations. It matters not whether the majority of your business is carried out via teleconferences, Video conference or in person, the same logic will still apply. Face to face however will normally be the most impactful but you must learn to see the same politics played out through other mediums.

The books main message is that in order to be effective and survive in this world you will need to become an expert in three interrelated areas; You will need to know your environment, know your opponent an above all know yourself. Once you have mastered these three areas, you will enjoy the corporate world like never before.

# Keywords

business psychology; stress management; conflict resolution; mediation; self-help; empowerment; self-realization; ego; leadership; mutualism; workplace conflict; interviews; classical game theory; evolutionary game theory; combat phycology; evolution; biology; statistical analysis; conflict studies; office politics; anthropomorphism; mimicry; aposematism; camouflage; project management; program management; skills development; careers management; performance review; leadership/management; hierarchy expectations; success criteria; written and oral communications; human behavior; drive; ambition; emotion; strategy

# Contents

Chapter 1    Introduction to the Corporate Jungle...................................1

The Jungle...........................................................................3

The Emergent Layer ......................................................4

The Canopy.....................................................................4

The Understory .............................................................4

The Forest Floor ...........................................................4

The Corporate Jungle ..........................................................5

Security Layer..................................................................7

Strategic Layer ................................................................8

Service Layer ..................................................................8

Specialist Layer ..............................................................9

Fruits of the Jungle............................................................11

Corporate Ladder...............................................................11

Chapter 2    Know Your Opponent.................................................13

The ID ...........................................................................19

The Ego .........................................................................19

The Superego .................................................................20

Personalities ....................................................................21

Amphibians.....................................................................22

Salamanders (Caudata) ................................................23

High Profile: Salamander: Mushroom-tongued

Salamanders (Bolitoglossa) .....................................24

Frogs and Toads (Anura)...............................................25

Toads..............................................................................26

Caecilians (Apoda)........................................................28

Reptiles ..........................................................................29

Snakes and Lizards (Squamites) ..................................30

Lizards (Squamata) .......................................................33

Turtles and Tortoises (Testudines).............................34

Crocodiles, Alligators, and Caimans (Crocodilians) ....36

Birds ........................................................................39
  Parrots (Psittaciformes) ...................................40
  Songbirds: (Passennes) ....................................42
  Pheasants, Peacocks, Chickens, and Turkeys
    (Galliformes)..............................................44
Birds of Prey...........................................................46
  Falcons (Falconiformes) ..................................46
  Eagles and Vultures (Accipitriformes) ..........48
  Eagles ...............................................................48
  Vultures............................................................49
  High Profile: King Vulture (Sarcoramphus papa)........50
Creepy Crawlies .....................................................51
  Spiders, Scorpions (Arachnids) .....................52
  Spiders..............................................................52
  Scorpions..........................................................54
Trapping a Scorpion..............................................55
  Centipedes, Millipedes (Myriapods) ............55
  Ants (Formicidea) ............................................57
  Bees (Apoidea) .................................................59
  Wasps and Hornets (Vespa) ...........................62
  Mosquitos and Flies (Diptera) .......................63
  Butterflies and Moths (*Including Caterpillars*)
    (Lepidoptera) .............................................65
  Snails and Slugs (Gastropods) ........................68
Fish .........................................................................70
  Cartilaginous Fish: Sharks and Rays
    (Chondrichthyes) .......................................71
  Sharks (Selachimorpha) ..................................71
  Rays (Batoidea)................................................73
  Bony Fish (Osteichthyes)................................75
  Piranha (Serrasalmidae) ..................................75
Mammals.................................................................77
  Rodents: Mice, Rats, Beavers (Rodentia) .....77
  Bats (Chiroptera).............................................80
  Shrews and Hedgehogs (Eulipotyphla) ........81
  Sloths and Anteaters (Pilosa)..........................83

Anteaters ....................................................83

Sloths .......................................................84

Hoofed Animals (ungulates) .............................87

Elephants (Elephantidae)................................89

Apes and Monkeys (Primates)..........................90

Great Apes.................................................91

Lesser Apes ...............................................93

Monkeys....................................................93

Prosimians.................................................94

Trapping a Primate...........................................96

Meat-Eating Predator Cats (Carnivora feliformia) ......96

Tigers (Panthera tigris) ..................................96

Sumatran Tigers (Panthera tigris sondaica) ...............96

Jaguars (Panthera onca) .................................98

Chapter 3    Know Your Environment .............................103

Unnatural Selection.........................................104

Game Theory...............................................111

Cooperative and Noncooperative Games....................112

Prisoner's Dilemma .........................................114

Social Dilemma.............................................116

Evolutionary Game Theory .................................117

Chapter 4    Know Yourself.........................................121

Before Entering the Jungle .................................122

Instinct versus Learned Behaviors..........................125

Systematic Desensitization .................................126

Cognitive Dissonance.......................................126

Denial......................................................127

Repression..................................................127

Stockholm Syndrome.......................................127

Displacement ...............................................128

Reaction Formation ........................................128

Stress.......................................................128

The Importance of Compasses..............................130

Success and Enemies .......................................130

Respect ....................................................131

Ambition ..................................................132

Chapter 5    Warfare ................................................................135
Corporate Psychological Warfare....................................136
Baiting ................................................................144
Camouflage................................................................146
Infrasound and Ultrasound .........................................150
False Retreats................................................................151
False Movements and Decoys....................................151
Trapping (Flypaper Theory) ........................................151
Gaslighting ................................................................152
Strategic Deterrents....................................................153
Operational Tactics ....................................................154
Natural Reluctance to Kill...........................................154
Prebattle Considerations .............................................159
Reconnaissance, Infiltration, and Espionage..................160
Ambush Strategy........................................................163
Summary ................................................................164
Ambush Tactics...........................................................164
Effective Counterinsurgency Methods..........................168
Positions with Increased Level of Difficulties.................173
Summary ................................................................175
Skirmishes................................................................175
Other Offensive Tactics Utilized by Opponents ...........176
Collateral Damage ......................................................178
Summary ................................................................178
False Flags ................................................................179
Effective Counterinsurgency Methods..........................179
Offensive Strategies and Tactics Used by
    You against Your Opponents....................................179
Strategies for Dealing with Difficult People...................181
Human Emotions ........................................................181
    Anxiety, Fear................................................182
    Disgust, Awkwardness .................................183
    Envy................................................................183
    Anger, Sadness.............................................184
Rivalries and Vendettas................................................186
Bullying ................................................................187

Identifying and Dealing with a Bully.............................187
Benefits and Limitations of Engaging HR.....................189
Defending Coworkers .................................................190
Hierarchies.................................................................191
     Unconsciously Inept Managers ...............................192
     Consciously Inept Managers...................................192
Winning by Not Winning.............................................195
Psychology of an Ambush ............................................197
Factors of Influence.....................................................198
Other Points to Consider in the Field...........................199
Chapter 6    Counterinsurgency Techniques for Organizations
             (for Natural Ecosystem Balance) .................................201
             Seven Golden Rules ......................................................202
             Propaganda ................................................................206

Bibliography...............................................................................209
About the Author........................................................................213
Formal Permissions Obtained for Quotations >100 Words.....................215
Index .........................................................................................225

# CHAPTER 1

# Introduction to the Corporate Jungle

*Non nobis solum nati sumus*
*(We are not born for ourselves alone.)*
Cicero, Roman Statesman 106–104 BC

The striking similarities between corporate workplaces and wild jungles cannot be denied.

Both environments typify intense competition, danger, fear, and, more importantly, cooperation.

We spend one-third of our 24-hour day at work, and 50% of our waking hours are dedicated to the office in pursuit of our economic means of survival—money.

In all tropical rain forests, competition underpins every interaction; from the trees competing for sunlight to the animals competing for food and territory, every day is a battle for survival.

The entire survival process, however, is underpinned by cooperation, which is often overlooked in the selfish pursuit of success, but in order to succeed in any of these environments, despite our best efforts, our success, like our fate, can often be beyond our control.

This is where we must learn to adapt our behaviors and actions and refine them to better increase our chances of survival when in any of these environments.

Let's look at how theories in relation to the elements of survival and competition have been presented throughout history.

In his most famous work *Principles of Population*, published in 1798, Economist Robert Malthus theorized that population growth in humans will always outstrip the level of necessary food required to feed each member of the population. This theory was influenced by current events surrounding the French Revolution (1789–1799) and is actually a sociopolitical commentary on that period, when the growth of the French population over time resulted in starvation and ultimately, unrest of the people. Malthus' work essentially theorized that even if food were secured and distributed equally to all members of the population, it would still run out because demand would always outstrip supply in relation to these finite resources. He theorized that while populations increased geometrically, food supply increased only arithmetically.

For example, when humans breed, they essentially multiply, and each population increase is via progressive multiplication, whereas food production cannot keep up with this rapid progression and can increase only by addition. So if population grows by a factor of two, it looks something like this:

2, 4, 8, 16, 32, 64, 128,

whereas food production, in keeping up with the demand at a factor of two, can progress only like this:

2, 4, 6, 8, 10, 12, 14, 16

Malthus concluded that in situations where population outstrips food supply, individuals within the population will compete against each other for the same resources or cooperate to locate new food sources and sometimes undertake a mixture of both.

Charles Darwin grew very interested in this approach and applied this methodology to the study of animals, culminating in his most famous work *The Origin of the Species*, published in 1859.

Darwin's pioneering book underpins the elements of competition and cooperation within the animal world and the struggle for survival.

These theories and methodologies lend themselves quite well to the corporate world, because, after all, humans have evolved from primates and share many traits.

Another area that lends itself quite well to the corporate world is guerrilla warfare, which is an attempt (or result) to ensure the survival of each participant by participating in a shared cause in the competition for resources, territory, or power. All three of these environments (the animal kingdom, guerrilla battlefields, and the corporate world) share a common environment in the jungle because each day has the same ultimate objective—survival.

## The Jungle

Entering a tropical jungle will usually evoke quite primordial feelings and thoughts. The intimidating ambience of the unknown, the sounds, smells, and tastes of a raw, wild unfamiliar environment can strike fear into the heart of even the bravest soul. Our natural human fear of the unknown will kick in, and you will instinctively be faced with the natural adrenaline rush that will genetically inform your next move.

The visual spectrum will be a green wall of impenetrable flora that you must hack your way through to successfully negotiate your entry. Owing to the lack of sunlight on the forest floor, you will not be able to see more than 6 feet ahead of you at all times, while strange animals will move above you and in every direction around you. It is not for the fainthearted.

Covering only 6 percent of the earth's surface, rain forests possess 50 percent of all the animal species on earth, so you are never too far away from your neighbors.

In the jungle you must remember that almost everything that you touch or see can cause you harm in many different ways, and you must therefore learn to distinguish what is safe to interact with from what is not.

In view of the physical dynamics of the jungle, where obstacles are constantly in your path, ambush is the only method of attack by all creatures because the lack of a clear passageway precludes a chase or a hunt, so danger will literally be lurking around every corner. That is easier said than done when there are no distinguishable corners…

To get a better handle on the environment, a simple graphic best explains the structure.

Throughout this book you will see the words "jungle" and "rain forest" used interchangeably; this is done intentionally to highlight or portray certain natural disciplines that attempt to bring order to the unknown.

*Figure 1.1 Graphic of rain forest layers*

The rain forest is made up of four layers:

## The Emergent Layer

This is the very top of the rain forest and contains the flora that has successfully won the sunlight race. These large trees have become the tallest in the entire ecosystem and receive the full effects of all weather before any other tree in the rain forest.

## The Canopy

This is the level directly below the emergent layer and is characterized by literally millions of trees; also known as the "roof of the rain forest," it contains high levels of humidity. At this level the temperatures are not as extreme, making this the perfect environment for fruit to grow. Because this is the layer of the rain forest that contains the most fruit, the highest diversity of animals is found here rather than at any of the other levels.

## The Understory

This is the level directly below the canopy, where temperatures are not as hot and fruit not as abundant; and it is where the younger, smaller trees can be found.

## The Forest Floor

This is the level that receives the least sunlight, with only 7 percent of the sun's rays reaching the forest floor on a daily basis, and, as a consequence, this level does not have much growth. Here is where leaf litter is broken down and recycled.

In addition to the preceding four main layers, there is also the river that sweeps alongside the ground level of the trees and that possesses its own unique characteristics. We will cover this further on in the book.

Despite having a basic grasp of the visual aesthetics of the four rain forest levels, it is imperative that you understand the four principles or guidelines rather that oddly regulate this wild environment.

First, you must understand that every creature in the jungle has a predator and that even those at the top of the food chain are vulnerable in their youth.

Second, you must understand that every living organism is connected or interlinked with every other living thing around it. Different species rely on each other for survival, whether they realize it or not, and every living member of the jungle has a purpose in the function that it serves and the ultimate impact that it has on its environment, whether it be deemed trivial or monumental.

Third, nothing goes to waste in the jungle; every living thing is re-cycled and reused over and over again.

And, fourth, you must understand that the jungle has a way of self-preservation and regulation that does not allow one species to domi-nate. If one species becomes too large or powerful and it is negatively impacting on others in the ecosystem, that dominant species will suc-cumb to an event or series of events that will naturally return balance to the ecosystem.

## The Corporate Jungle

Entering a corporate environment for the first time, as in the case of the jungle, can also be an unnerving affair.

You will naturally try to find your bearings when you are faced first with the visual spectacle of rows and rows of cubicles that are indistin-guishable from each other. Once you have been introduced to a multitude of different corporate animals within an extremely short space of time, you will then be shown to your desk. When seated, your visibility is re-duced to merely a few feet in front of you as a wall of gray felt blinkers you to focus your attention on the luminous screen that sits directly in front of you. You will hear noises from all around you in every direction, some hostile, some friendly, and some that you just cannot work out at all. The smell of perfume or aftershave will consume your senses and disorientate you as you get used to this new environment. You will not be able to decipher friend from foe, and you will normally avoid any unwanted attention until you have a better handle on the culture and inner workings of this strange new land.

Like the jungles of the southern hemisphere, many species in the corporate office are deadly and see you as either predator or prey. Even if you are not their predator, just being a predator will normally imply that they see you as their competition, but their intentions will not be obvious at such an early stage; hence, over time you must learn to distinguish between who is safe and who is not and take care not to succumb to paranoia and conspiracy theories relating to their motivations without solid evidence.

Given the physical dynamics of the corporate environment, as in the jungle, where obstacles are constantly in your path, ambush is the only method of attack by all creatures, so you will not normally see your enemies coming.

Similarly to the wild jungle, the corporate jungle will normally have its own set of principles, guidelines, or regulations that senior leaders see as being of grave importance to the upkeep of the environment.

These will normally be referred to as "corporate values" and will quite normally be indistinguishable from organization to organization, because many core values seem to always be shared.

They will usually focus on communication, customer first, collaboration, integrity, trust, and so forth.

Some organizations actually follow these and hold them in high regard, but many don't and ultimately operate independently of these values and view them as preselected imposed codes of morality on display for promotional purposes alone.

In addition to these core values, which are often designed to be reflected internally as well as externally, organizations will often be bound by a process referred to as "corporate social responsibility (CSR)," which is a code of behavior designed to regulate its overall impact on the wider external environment.

CSR principles normally include ecological promises and focus on areas that the corporation intends to assist in, such as helping an area of disadvantaged society or grouping.

Again, the adherence to these principles will vary between corporations because many entities can try to capitalize on these promises and use them as public relations stunts. Which companies actually adhere to these principles and which do not will become evident as time goes by.

The corporate jungle also mirrors the four different layers of the rain forest, but it is important to note that these layers are not levels and are most definitely not four grades of a corporate hierarchy that ranks each layer in levels of ascending importance. You must understand, rather, that each layer is an individual part of a wider whole with hierarchies endemic within each layer only and not normally against other layers.

Each animal has a specific set of skills that allow it to operate effectively in each layer, and it is in these specific areas that it thrives the most.

The corporate jungle can best be differentiated by four distinct but interlinked areas, known as the **four S's.**

*Figure 1.2  Rainforest layers overlaid with 4 "S" levels*

*Security Layer*

This is the layer that ensures that corporate governance is being upheld but that also seeks to protect the organization from any oncoming attacks either from within or without. Employees in this category pay keen attention to detail and are extremely knowledgeable about current internal and external pieces of legislation with passageway navigated in a shrewd way in order to protect the company's best interests. In order to effectively undertake these roles to the best of their abilities, however, animals that dwell in this layer are adapted with flight or powerful climbing skills to ensure that they can view great distances in front of them and gain the best possible perspective of their environment. Animals at this level are adapted to endure the heat and are safe from distractions to concentrate on the necessary tasks at hand.

**Functions within this layer**: Legal, Finance, Human Resources, Internal audit, PR and Marketing

**Animals within this layer**: Birds of Prey

### Strategic Layer

This is the layer of the organization that contains the highest diversity of animals because it yields the highest rewards. Animals residing in this layer of the rain forest are responsible for the maximum seed dispersal in the organization as they go about their daily routines. In the corporate world, these animals are responsible for the strategic direction of the organization, ensuring that the company is always moving to a place of betterment and safety, and they must therefore be agile.

They set policies and standards aimed at keeping the organization on course and that the rest of the organization must adhere to, and therefore they are normally experts in their field. You must also be aware that competition is fierce within this layer and that it is characterized by more politics than any other level. Animals that make mistakes at this level can fall, with only half of monkey species in the wild making it to adulthood owing to the falls that they encounter.

**Functions within this layer**: Infrastructure Asset Management, Project Management, Change Management, IT, Scientists

**Animals within this layer:** Monkeys

### Service Layer

This layer of the corporate jungle is the engine room, where all the tangible output takes place.

Animals adapted to this area thrive under pressure and are driven by the successful conclusions of their endeavors, resulting in output that they can see and touch, such as an end product or service completion.

**Functions within this layer:** Operations, Engineers, Sales staff, Stock market traders

**Animals within this layer:** Honeybees

### Specialist Layer

This layer of the corporate rain forest contains the most innovative employees, who are usually the founders of many organizations or creators of initiatives.

Owing to the lack of sunlight and growth, those that dwell within this area must successfully innovate within these constraints in order to be successful and see potential in places where nobody thinks that it is possible. Only those adapted to this area can survive because it contains some of the most resilient creatures who are open to change and who will therefore always look for ways to be successful in times of hardship.

**Functions within this layer:** CEO's, Research and Development (R&D)

**Animals within this layer:** Jaguars, Anteaters

When comparing the wild and corporate jungles it is useful to draw a comparison between the wildlife present in each environment with that in the other. Anthropomorphism is a process whereby human features or behaviors are applied to animals which can best interpret or display a specific set of actions or behaviors

Every cartoon, novel, and Disney animated feature film portrays anthropomorphism to its audiences and is a useful way to display animal emotions and behavior to a wider audience.

Ethology is a branch of biological science that investigates the cognitive abilities of animals and has produced some extremely interesting and awe-inspiring results.

Jane Goodall, in her interactions with primates, attests to the human traits that these creatures exhibit that have informed our understanding of these animals far beyond our previous level of awareness.

Marc Bekoff, in his book, *The Emotional Lives of Animals,* shares compelling instances of animal cognitive abilities and humanlike emotions dealing with elephants that grieve and canines and even serpents that display unrelenting loyalty toward their owners. These remarkable tales all point to the fact that animals are emotional sentient beings that display humanlike behaviors, but reading and interpreting animal behavior and understanding their motivations is a lot easier than understanding human behavior. Animals cannot hide their emotions as humans can, and these wild honest displays of emotion can help us understand human nature somewhat better.

When navigating the corporate jungle environment, it is important that you learn to interpret patterns and activities that will assist you in your interactions within this environment.

The first aspect of awareness is knowing what time of the day is the most effective for getting a task completed either by yourself or with the assistance of others.

For example, the cooler air present within jungles in the early morning allows sounds to travel farther than at any other time of day because sounds made in the mid- to late afternoon are muffled by the hot dense air that transcends this environment; furthermore, although sounds can also travel far in the evening, it is not normally advised to pursue tasks after the working day is over.

A key lesson to note, therefore, is that activities undertaken in the early morning will usually be the most productive and impactful. This is mirrored in the corporate jungle, where engaging someone in the early morning will ensure that they are fresh and at their most productive, whereas if you engage them in the late afternoon there is a greater chance that they will be worn down from the interactions that have already taken place up to that point and that your message or intentions can be easily misinterpreted or misunderstood. The key is to strike while people are at their most motivated, so early morning meetings are always preferred to late afternoon meetings.

In chapter three of this book, we shall go on to examine the corporate jungle further and discuss how best to adapt in order to survive in this wilderness.

You must also appreciate that jungles are essentially self-sufficient ecosystems that regulate their own weather. The hot temperatures that cause evaporation result in an overabundance of water vapor constantly present in the air, which also causes high humidity. This water vapor is then spread by wind and results in a deluge of rainfall all over the environment.

Corporate jungles are no different in that they essentially strive to create the optimum environment that can cause growth, just as water is seen as the lifeblood of the jungle and as key to its ultimate survival. The corporate jungle, however, can create its own storms that are normally political in nature.

Another important area of advice when navigating the wild jungle is understanding how your physical and mental condition play a somewhat obvious part in your resilience and ability to survive. You must be aware that many flora and fauna can be extremely toxic or venomous and will have detrimental effects on your health. In addition to the pain caused by these interactions, these toxic elements will usually manifest themselves as stress and fatigue in the corporate jungle. You must therefore be able to recognize these effects and take stock of its impact on your performance and ultimate well-being. Take care not to let awareness of your own personal weaknesses and strengths be clouded by ego so that you are not overwhelmed by any encounter within this environment. You must seek to find your place within each of the four layers of the corporate jungle.

## Fruits of the Jungle

In the pursuit of goals and rewards within the corporate jungle, you must recognize that there is always more than one species competing in this endeavor. This is nature's way of selecting the strongest species and ensuring the "survival of the fittest," as espoused by Charles Darwin.

Competition will usually involve many political and psychological battles, so you must thoroughly assess your strategy in relation to your quest and not rush headfirst into a situation without carefully assessing your options.

Once a goal has been developed into a plausible strategy, you must be aware of the routes to success and the pitfalls that can lie along the journey. The first lesson you must learn is the myth of the corporate ladder.

## Corporate Ladder

It must be stressed that the idea of, or preoccupation with, a corporate ladder is a complete fallacy.

Climbing a ladder is futile if you are an elephant that wants to reach the emergent level of the rain forest to live with the eagles.

Progression in the jungle is along a horizontal albeit zigzag path, so career progression is more akin to running the gauntlet, attacked from every direction by opponents.

Another adaptation critical for success in both the wild and corporate jungles is camouflage, or the ability to blend into your environment to either attack prey or hide from a predator. All inhabitants of both the wild and the corporate jungles must learn to conceal their presence in order to ensure their survival.

Animals in the wild jungle do this effectively by having stripes, spots, and even colorations identical to those of their surroundings. Animals in the corporate jungle do this by wearing professional work attire. Wearing suitable attire in the office will ensure that you do not unnecessarily stand out or attract unwanted attention, because there is normally a minimum accepted level of tolerance of this rule to ensure a climate of conformance that is in line with the organization's culture.

Essentially, corporate dress codes are a uniform which ensures a specific subconscious state of mind in the wearer in the same way that combat attire or military fatigues symbolize to the soldier that they are entering battle. We will discuss this further in the course of the book.

# CHAPTER 2

# Know Your Opponent

*Fas est ab hoste doceri*
*(One should learn, even from one's enemies.)*

Ovid, Roman Poet 43 BC–17AD

In this section, I will attempt to surmise the different types of animals that you will encounter within the corporate jungle. I have done this by observing the animals' behavior in the wild and have attempted to establish their motivations and, ultimately, their personalities.

As stated in the previous chapter, the wild jungle contains fierce competition for every resource, and the corporate jungle is no different, so you must know your opponent and never underestimate them.

I am also making a distinction between "opponent" and "enemy," because having an enemy implies some level of history and emotion that is not always characteristic of attacks within the corporate jungle, where some acts of aggression are unconscious and therefore not personal. Some of the most horrendous attacks in the corporate world are carried out in a cold, unforgiving manner and do not possess the heat that is normally associated with emotional battles.

Many opponents can also become fierce rivals, so it is important to know your opponent before they become your enemy.

*If you know the enemy and know yourself, you need not fear the result of a hundred battles. If you know yourself but not the enemy, for every victory gained you will also suffer a defeat. If you know neither the enemy nor yourself, you will succumb in every battle.*

Sun Tzu (*The Art of War*)

When dealing with opponents it is important to understand that psychology permeates every motivation, decision, and action that they make.

Organizations are fiercely political environments, and the rule is that an individual must be more adept at political prowess with every increase in seniority that they achieve. Politics appear, however, at every level of organizations, but the necessity and criticality of masking politics also increase in relation to the seniority of the person's role.

We have all heard the terms **Sociopath, Psychopath, Machiavellian, Narcissist, and Egocentric** used within the workplace to describe someone or other, but what do they actually mean, and are they being used in the correct context?

Let's first look at the terms "sociopath" and "psychopath." Both terms actually relate to a condition that is a diagnosable mental illness.

They are both known as antisocial personality disorders (APD), so someone is not medically diagnosed as being a definitive "sociopath" or a definitive "psychopath" because they are both grouped under one umbrella.

A look at the National Health Service's (NHS) website gives information on this condition:

*Antisocial personality disorder: Personality disorders are mental health conditions that affect how someone thinks, perceives, feels, or relates to others.*

www.nhs.uk

So this condition affects how someone thinks, perceives, feels, or relates to others? This is interesting, so are there any distinguishable traits or characteristics?

The website continues:

*Signs of antisocial personality disorder: A person with antisocial personality disorder may:*

- *Exploit, manipulate or violate the rights of others*
- *Lack concern, regret or remorse about people's distress*
- *Behave irresponsibly and show disregard for normal social behavior*

- *Have difficulty sustaining long-term relationships*
- *Be unable to control their anger*
- *Lack guilt or not learn from their mistakes*
- *Blame others for problems in their lives*
- *Repeatedly break the law*

www.nhs.uk

So now we know the characteristics, but how is it treated or cured?

*Evidence suggests behaviour can improve over time with therapy, even if core characteristics such as lack of empath remain. But antisocial personality disorder is one of the most difficult types of personality disorders to treat. A person with antisocial personality disorder may also be reluctant to seek treatment and may only start therapy when ordered to do so by a court.*

www.nhs.uk

That, essentially, leaves three avenues for people with APD:

1. They are forced to attend therapy by a court against their will.
2. They seek help themselves by their own free will.
3. They never seek help but manage to "function" by keeping their impulses and behaviors at such a level as not to break the law.

Let's face it, the difficult person in your office who has been there for a long time is probably more than likely going to remain there. So you must remember that when dealing with difficult people, there is a good chance that you are actually dealing with a verifiable mental illness.

Not that this fact will make it any easier to endure; it simply highlights that it is not the person that you are dealing with in these encounters but the demons within them. Care must also be taken not to label or diagnose these illnesses, because they are diagnosed only by trained medical professionals. I merely highlight them here to illustrate that there may be much more to an issue than meets the eye.

Let's move on now to the term "Machiavellian"; I'm sure you've heard this phrase used around the office in reference to someone who has schemed an underhanded self-serving plan. This is in the ballpark of correctness but does not capture the true power of the phrase or indeed the concept.

The term Machiavellian derives from the 16th century Italian diplomat, author, and political advisor Niccolo Machiavelli and his most famous book, *The Prince*, which depicts all the necessary strategies a ruler must adhere to in order to rule appropriately.

The book has some controversial points and learnings but has been held in some infamy for over 500 years.

The book essentially claims that it is impossible to be a good politician and a nice person at the same time. This sounds harsh, but let's explore this further: Machiavelli is saying that in order to effectively make the right decisions that will benefit either self-preservation and/or the wider population, you must make sacrifices that will cut across and conflict with your virtues. He actually goes farther than that and exclaims: "It is better to be feared than loved if you cannot be both."

He informs the reader that there is a side to us all that is normally hidden but must be shown sometimes: "Everyone sees what you appear to be, few experience what you really are."

These guidelines relate to achieving power, but he goes on to advise strategies for holding on to success and power:

"If an injury has to be done to a man it should be so severe that his vengeance need not be feared."

It is quite easy to draw parallels between Machiavellian strategies and theories and the corporate world.

The political nature of business lends itself perfectly to Machiavellian theories and can possibly answer some of those burning questions as to why your leaders are being so cold and uncaring toward a specific issue or cause. The reason is that they are either desensitized or in the process of desensitizing, and their behavior is merely self-preservation behavior achieved through a practiced technique.

It can also explain why that nice, amicable employee changed on getting a promotion: They too are practicing self-preservation techniques because their new role does not allow them to be accommodating and effective at the same time.

You must therefore understand that politics play a critical role in your success and survival in the corporate world, but you must be aware of when they are at odds with your morals. Sometimes ignorance is bliss, but compromising your morals will always ultimately affect you in ways that you least consider.

Let's move on now on to the term "narcissist." Believe it or not, Narcissism is also a verifiable medical condition and is categorized as another personality disorder.

Let's look at the medical definition of this condition from the Mayo clinic:

*Narcissistic personality disorder, one of several types of personality disorders, is a mental condition in which people have an inflated sense of their own importance, a deep need for excessive attention and admiration, troubled relationships and a lack of empathy for others. But behind this mask of extreme self-confidence lies a fragile self-esteem that's vulnerable to the slightest criticism.*

Mayo clinic (www.mayoclinic.org)

Ok… so what are the symptoms and signs to look out for…

*Signs and symptoms of narcissistic personality disorder and the severity of symptoms vary.*

*People with the disorder can*

- *Have an exaggerated sense of self importance*
- *Have a sense of entitlement and require constant, excessive admiration*
- *Expect to be recognised as superior even without achievements that warrant it*
- *Exaggerate achievements and talents*
- *Believe they are superior and can only associate with equally special people*
- *Monopolise conversations and belittle or look down on people they perceive as inferior*
- *Take advantage of others to get what they want*
- *Be envious of others and believe others envy them*

Mayo clinic (www.mayoclinic.org)

Ok, so is there anything else we should know…?

*People with narcissistic personality disorders have trouble handling any-thing they perceive as criticism, and they can:*

- *Become impatient or angry when they don't get special attention*
- *React with rage or contempt and try to belittle the other person to make themselves appear superior*
- *Have difficulty regulating emotions and behavior*
- *Have secret feelings of insecurity, shame, vulnerability, and humiliation* Mayo clinic (www.mayoclinic.org)

I'm sure you will all know or have known someone like that in your lives. Dealing with people who exhibit these traits is indeed difficult, but, again, you must be aware that when dealing with people like this you are dealing with a mental illness. Identical to ASD mentioned above, simply being aware of these fact will not make it any easier to endure; it simply highlights that it is not the person that you are dealing with in these encounters but the demons within them. Again as with ASD mentioned above, care must also be taken not to label or diagnose these illnesses because they are diagnosed only by trained medical professionals; I high-light them here merely to illustrate that there may be much more to an issue than meets the eye.

OK, let's move on to the ego! What really is an ego? The *Cambridge Dictionary* gives the follow definition:

*Ego: Your idea or opinion of yourself, especially your feeling of your own importance and ability*

OK, so your ego is essentially how your view yourself; I understand that part, but what about "your feelings of your self-importance and abil-ity" part?

Well, if I view myself as a king, I will expect everyone to treat me as one, and, conversely, if I view myself as a peasant, I would expect every-one to treat me as a peasant.

The ego therefore cuts across self-esteem and self-confidence, all of which are intertwined.

Let's take the example of someone viewing themselves as a king; they will therefore expect to be treated as a king. Why is this so? Surely, a king does not require validation from anyone else to reinforce his kingliness? Well, that is correct if you really are a king, but one who just views oneself as a king is obviously not a real king and so will require validation along the way in order to keep up the premise. The constant need for validation exposes a weakness within the individual, because if the constant validation is not forthcoming, they will become agitated.

Corporate egos can be the most difficult egos to encounter on the planet. Why? Because there are so many of them sharing a small space. Every day is a battle of egos, with everyone demanding to be treated like kings and queens and recognized as masters of their own domain or territories.

Recognition, therefore, plays a key part in ego; the king must be recognized as one on every possible occasion, with the ego defining their ultimate personality and how they are viewed by others.

Let's look at the psychological definition of "ego" in order to gain a better understanding of its makeup and abilities.

Sigmund Freud, the father of psychology, theorized three parts that define a person's personality. He categorized these as the *ID*, the *Ego,* and the *Superego.*

## The ID

The ID is the most basic part of our human personalities and is present from birth. It represents our subconscious basic urges, which if not met instantly will cause distress. Examples include a child who is hungry and wants to be fed instantly. They will cry and scream until their hunger is satisfied.

## The Ego

The Ego forms when we become older and more self-aware and is the part of our personality that tries to make the demands of the ID acceptable or reasonable to society. Taking the example of the hungry child again, now the adult is hungry but will not cry and scream or indeed scoff sandwiches during a workplace presentation because the adult knows that this is not socially acceptable.

# The Superego

This third part of the human personality is always the last to develop and is focused solely on morals.

The superego differs from the ego in that the ego deals only with social perceptions, but the superego is concerned with doing the right thing. This is essentially how a conscience is formed.

This can all be summed up very easily:

- ID is impressing no one (unconscious)
- Ego is impressing others
- Superego is impressing yourself

What this reveals is that a personality is a tripartite condition made up of unconscious and conscious elements that all come together to make a functioning human being, but they are not easily defined and are sometimes in direct conflict with each other.

What this also reveals is that the portrayal of the "ego" in the vernacular as a negative thing is not necessarily correct. The ego is essentially the component of your personality that tries to regulate the unconscious ID, so it has a fully valid and important role to play in our personalities.

The issue arises, however, when someone's "ID," "Ego," or "Superego" is out of balance.

There will be situations within a person's development that will both consciously and subconsciously change or shape their views on life.

The ego, as stated, is constantly trying to keep the "ID" at bay, so if there is a stronger "ID," it will result in someone seeking to satisfy their basic urges all the time, which will result in probably jail or some sort of trouble; therefore, the "ego" is essentially a defense mechanism.

The ID also negatively affects the superego because the instant gratification is sometimes required by the morally superior superego, and this is where the ego must intervene in order to make it socially acceptable.

A stronger superego will lead to a person displaying extremely judgmental or holier than thou attitudes, which will also have a negative effect on a person's image.

If the ego itself is the stronger component of the three, it results in the person constantly seeking validation from society to compensate for their basic ID urges. It will also affect the superego because morals will be imbalanced, with some detriment to the person's thoughts, actions, and ultimate survival.

So the ego is not a bad thing, but an imbalanced ego most definitely is.

Okay, we have looked at how different factors make up and affect people's personalities and have discussed the definitions of these terms. We will revisit this in chapter five, where I will explain how best to deal with people who exhibit these personality traits. But before that we must first seek to discover what type of people you will meet in every office to best discover which ones are more prone to displaying these behavioral traits.

## Personalities

When looking to observe and record personality traits, researchers Naomi Takemoto-chock, Lewis Goldberg, Andrew Comrey, and John Digman, in the 1980s, advanced a model that had been developed by various academic minds, entitled the "Big five personality traits." These five traits underpin each individual personality and determine their dominance.

These are characterized by the acronym O-C-E-A-N

1. **O: Openness to experience**
   This trait encompasses the natural curiosity about the environment and the willingness of pursuit in new experiences or encounters.
2. **C: Conscientiousness**
   This is the level of thoughtfulness, insight, and self-awareness displayed by individuals.
3. **E: Extraversion**
   This involves the level of sociability and expressions of outgoing behavior displayed by an individual.
4. **A: Agreeableness**
   This is the level of altruism or cooperation displayed by individuals.
5. **N: Neuroticism**
   This trait encompasses the level of instability or insecurity that a person displays.

I have attempted to apply the foregoing methodology to the animal kingdom in an attempt to learn from an honest and pure form of these displayable traits. Animals cannot hide their emotions or personalities as humans do, so a study of their behavior is critical in seeking to understand our own.

The following is a list of animals that can be found in the corporate jungle.

*Note: I have specifically opted to use harmless trapping techniques over harmful hunting techniques so as to effectively expose your opponents whom you need to catch alive, and, in addition, I'm an animal lover and only advocate a catch and rerelease policy.*

## Amphibians

Office Amphibians are a diverse species and play a key role in organizational upkeep.

Amphibians, having thin skin, are affected by subtle changes to their environment. These groups are referred to in the wild as "bioindicator species," which means that their presence, numbers, and behavior are an indication of how toxic an environment is.

"Amphibian" stems from the Greek word *amphibios,* meaning "to have a double life" ("amphi" meaning "both kinds," and "bios" meaning "life"); amphibians adapt to their environment through developmental changes in order to live in water and on land, making them an extremely versatile species.

This versatility, applied in the office environment, allows office amphibians to adapt to altered demands and receive the esteem of senior management owing to their unique abilities in keeping the corporation on course.

Office amphibians are cold-blooded creatures and therefore do not display the warmth that is sometimes expected in a professional encounter. Empathy and sympathy are nonexistent in these creatures, and they have the ability to be extremely dangerous if not approached or managed in the correct manner. It must be noted, however, in regard to the difference between being toxic and being venomous, that while both characteristics are extremely dangerous, the latter implies a medium of transmission such as teeth or a stinger, whereas the former denotes that transmission of poison is obtained only when handled or touched. Amphibians, therefore, are toxic but not venomous.

Office amphibians can be grouped into three subcategories:

1. **Salamanders** (*Caudata*)
2. **Frogs and Toads** (*Anura*)
3. **Caecilians** (*Gymnophiona and Apoda*)

## *Salamanders (Caudata)*

Corporate salamanders are found in all organizations and are characterized by their semipermeable skin, which results in the absorption of toxins from their environment, so their mood will reflect the culture of the organization. Having thin skin, however, also makes them overly sensitive to criticism and prone to stress, so they do not work very well in highly stressful environments.

These small animals make barely audible noises so as not to be noticed and normally move quite quickly throughout the office.

They are determined creatures and will be meticulous in their work life activities. They will have a keen attention to detail and when things do not go to plan will panic and need reassurance.

It is important to note that all salamanders, as well as being bioindicators of the toxicity of the office environment, are also toxic themselves—toxic in a way, however, that is harmful not to themselves but to others when you either attack or spend too much time with them.

Salamander mucus contain a deadly chemical that when ingested can be fatal, so they should not be handled or attacked. Office salamanders have an affinity for details and facts, prefer routine, and normally hold positions that deal with corporate governance or finances.

When under threat or when pursued for wrongdoing, salamanders have the ability to shed their tails and regenerate limbs, making them somewhat resilient to blame and allowing them to deal with punishment from senior management very well and emerge relatively unscathed.

In general, the older the salamander, the fewer attackers it will have, because older salamanders are more toxic than younger salamanders and have built up a venom over the years in the office and have seen it all. Be cautious when engaging in battle with an older salamander.

Salamanders are mainly water-dwelling creatures, and this therefore means that to find an office salamander you will need to go looking in their specific department and that they will not always be easy to track down. You must go to them; they will never come to you, and they will appear only when they need to.

### High Profile: Salamander: Mushroom-tongued Salamanders (Bolitoglossa)

These aquatic dwelling creatures are notorious for their mushroom-shaped tongue, which is adapted to snatch prey in mere milliseconds. Another clever survival adaptation is their behavior within conflict situations. They remain still and wait for predators to make their first move; and once the salamander is touched by the attacker, they render the predator paralyzed by means of the deadly toxins on their skin, allowing ample time to retreat.

Dealing with a Salamander

Dealing with a salamander is a tricky affair because you can never touch them in view of their toxicity, and so interacting with them is a dangerous task. Owing to their governance and "policelike" enforcement positions within organizations, it is advisable to give them the information that they require and in the format in which they desire, ensuring that they are satisfied. Corporate salamanders do not like radical ways of doing things and are opposed to many innovative ideas and behaviors, so always adhere to their standardization, even when you know better. Unnecessarily taking on a salamander in order to prove a point is simply not worth the hassle.

Trapping a Salamander

However, there may be instances when you need to trap a salamander. No matter what the reason is, it is strongly advisable to take the necessary precautions. They best way to trap a salamander in the wild is to use a funnel trap, and this is no different when dealing with corporate salamanders.

Essentially, a funnel trap is a cylindrical meshlike object with two entrances but no exits, so when a creature enters the trap it is unable to escape because of the design of the object. Salamanders are keen burrowers and like to reside in crevices and burrow holes in order to feel safe. This trap design takes advantage of this behavior and uses the salamander's innate characteristics to trap themselves.

The corporate equivalent is sending the salamander on a self-edifying quest by laying snippets of information for them to find. This is, essentially, leading them on a journey away from you and focusing their attention on other activities, which will then overwhelm and disorientate them. This should be done not to divert attention to any illicit activities or governance breaches, but only to get a salamander off your back when you are overwhelmed.

### *Frogs and Toads* (**Anura**)

Office frogs are the second largest species of amphibians found in the office.

Like salamanders (and indeed all amphibians), frogs are bioindicators of the level of toxicity in an organization and held in high regard by senior management owing to their meticulous work ethic and their close attention to corporate governance. Office frogs keep the insect population under control and allow the organization to clearly operate either financially or operationally.

Frogs are social creatures and socialize in large groups. Office frogs, however, often form cliques and can be found sitting together in the canteen at lunch or break times engaging in gossip.

They also have unique behaviors, such as drinking differently than everyone else (through their skin), so they keep to themselves, but their interactions can appear quite unnatural from afar.

Frogs, like all amphibians, have slimy skin, and this can be quite disconcerting when interacting with a frog, but do not always conflate the sliminess with insincerity. As off-putting as the slimy demeanor may be, the sliminess displayed by frogs is merely an adaptation to survive in the office environment. It keeps their skin moist and allows them to function effectively. They are, however, slippery and hard to get a handle on. Frogs can also be severely poisonous, so it is advisable not to handle them when you do not know their species.

The tongue of a frog can snap and recoil at 15/100th of a second, making them masters of oral attacks; they will be harshly sarcastic and cutting with their words and seek sanctuary in their position within the company. Office frogs normally have a demeanor of arrogance and superiority but often know their place within the overall hierarchy.

### Toads

It is important to stress that all Toads are Frogs but not all Frogs are Toads. The main differences are that most toads live on land, whereas frogs don't venture too far from a water source. Toads have dry, bumpy skin, unlike frogs, which have a thin semipermeable skin, making them tougher and more resilient to criticism and stress.

Toads are also solitary creatures, so you will not see them in the canteen having coffee with the other office frogs. They tend to keep themselves to themselves. They are, however, quite poisonous and use this poison to ward off potential predators, so caution must also be employed when interacting with a toad.

High Profile: Golden Poison Dart Frog (*Phyllobates terribilis*)

This species of frog, native to the Columbian rain forest, is the most venomous amphibian on the planet. At just under 2 inches in height, its poison affects the nervous system of its victims and leads to sudden death. One frog can kill up to 20 human beings at once.

Dealing with a Frog

Frogs command high levels of respect in corporations, and the more of them that there are, the better the indication of the corporation's health and subsequent image. This fact, as mentioned earlier, can lead to arrogance within many corporate species, so dealing with an office frog will be a challenge. They will portray a conceited "holier than thou" attitude, exposing their knowledge of corporate governance and regulations, and will look to upstage you at every turn. Knowing this, however, allows you be one step ahead and allows you to play to their egos in order to achieve what you require from the interaction to get a task completed. They feed off compliments, and the old phrase "you can catch more flies with honey than with vinegar" is very apt here.

Trapping a Frog

Owing to their high levels of toxicity, they can be extremely dangerous, so engaging a frog is no easy feat. In the wild they are caught using a device known as a drift fence. A drift fence is merely a large vertical barrier in the ground that blocks a frog's path; the frog will then instinctively follow the perimeter of the fence in an attempt to get around it but then falls into one of two strategically placed pit traps dug at each end of the fence.

This can also be utilized effectively on corporate frogs because they will instinctively follow rules and regulations, which can be exploited in order to steer and divert their attention in order to catch or expose them.

## Caecilians (Apoda)

Caecilians are the most elusive of the amphibian family; even now in 2020 not a lot is known about their habits and behaviors. They are large wormlike creatures, sometimes reaching up to 5 feet in length, and live underground, coming to the surface only at night or after a heavy rainfall.

Caecilians, which are conditioned to living underground, have lost the ability of sight; even the word "caecilian" comes from the Latin word for blind (*caeus*); nevertheless, they are extremely determined creatures in what we know that they do—burrowing. Caecilians are expert tunnelers and burrowers and use their head to force their ways through the earth.

Office caecilians are no different, being extremely headstrong, hard to manage, and determined to plough through situations with no recourse. They are unknown to many in the office, or if they are known their day-to-day activities are a mystery. People may see them as being extremely busy, but the question is, busy doing what? Their lack of sight results in their being unable to assess the appropriate direction or impact on projects, and they cannot adhere to deadlines or timelines.

They are extremely elusive and cannot be contacted. They possess the same innate characteristics as other amphibian species, but they are toxic, slimy, and cold-blooded, so caution is always advised.

High Profile: Thomson's Caecilian (*Caecilia Thompsoni*)

Native to the Colombian rain forest, the Caecilia Thompsoni (or Thomson's Caecilian) is 5 feet in length and weighs just under 2 kg, making it the largest caecilian ever recorded.

Dealing with a Caecilian

Dealing with a caecilian is an extremely frustrating task because they are very difficult to find, and even once found, they are slippery creatures and very difficult to get a hold on. Placing trust in a caecilian to complete a task is fraught with danger because they will blindly pursue initiatives and not think outside the box. They will not adhere to deadlines and governance, and it is advisable to set out clearly any objectives that are necessary for success to the caecilian. It is also advisable to keep a written record of all requirements and interaction with a caecilian, not merely to inform the caecilian but to let more senior managers know who is responsible for task failures.

Trapping a Caecilian

Despite their elusive nature, it is actually quite easy to trap a caecilian. In the wild, they come to the surface only to eat after a heavy rainfall. They can easily be caught by being flushed out and overwhelmed with tasks within the corporate world. Despite being bulldozers in any task, once they feel lost or overwhelmed, however, they will frantically surface to seek redirection and then get caught. So the key is to overwhelm them with information and facts.

# Reptiles

Reptiles can be found in every workplace. They are a species that has existed for millions of years and naturally thrive in corporate environments because of their self-centered behavior. They are cold-blooded and prosper in hot climates because heat is necessary to be able to function.

Like office amphibians, they lack empathy and sympathy but differ in personalities.

Reptiles, being self-serving, every action is measured and carried out only to preserve their condition or position within the company. A reptile will do you a favor only if it gets something in return or if it can benefit from it directly.

Other office workers are wary of reptiles, more so than of other species, because they do not fully trust their behavior. Their abilities are not in question but merely their approach to business. Reptiles will throw anyone under the bus to get ahead in life, a ruthlessness that is sometimes rewarded in certain corporations.

Office reptiles can be grouped into three subcategories:

1. **Snakes and Lizards** (*Squamites*)
2. **Turtles and Tortoises** (*Testudines*)
3. **Crocodiles and Caimans** (*Crocodilians*)

### Snakes and Lizards (Squamites)

Snakes (*Serpentes*)

Office snakes are one of the deadliest species in any organization. Many species are venomous and extremely dangerous to all animals. Adapted for hunting, snakes possess special adapatations in their eyes, which sense heat given off by warm-blooded prey and can even sense vibrations from prey close by.

They use their tongues to smell and can sense the actual direction a smell is coming from. They can see and smell you coming and can strike you before you have registered what has happened. Not having a sense of taste, however, they do not discriminate in regard to choice of meal, and whatever food is in their way will do just fine, providing it can be swallowed.

Office snakes are no strangers to conflict but will often back down when confronted. Snakes are most vulnerable after a meal because their movement is restricted.

An office snake's reputation will precede it, and all peers and coworkers will be uneasy in its presence. They are often given a wide berth in contentious situations because many fear reprisals if they confront them. Snakes kill prey not just by venom but also by constriction; they will literally crush you to death and swallow you whole in order to get ahead in the organisation.

Snakes almost always reach senior management positions because their ruthlessness will achieve profits and results but at the cost of personal relationships and team spirit.

## High Profile Snake: South American Rattlesnake
## (Crotalus durissus)

Native to the Amazon rain forest in Brazil, the South American Rattlesnake is one of the most venomous species of snake in the world, and a bite from this snake can cause blindness, paralysis, and ultimately death. The venom contains deadly neurotoxins, and a victim who manages to survive will have lasting effects for many years thereafter.

## Dealing with a Snake

Dealing with a snake is not for the fainthearted. They can strike in any direction at any second, can dominate most prey, and will attack anyone that crosses their path.

Corporate snakes are no different and are constantly evaluating and assessing you, so when interacting with a snake it is important not to show weakness or give much more away than what the specific situation merits. Snakes will look for any angle in a situation that they can exploit and use to their advantage. They will often play to your emotions and get you riled up in order to achieve their objectives. Once they have you where they want you, they will strike.

Being aware of snake behavior is simply not enough to gain the upper hand, because enduring their behavior can significantly affect your mental health. They are an extremely psychological species and will make you second guess yourself at every turn, so in order to effectively deal with a snake you must stick to professionalism, not befriend them or let them inside your head, and keep every interaction rigid and succinct. Always keep to the facts while avoiding talk of feelings.

Just like the snake handlers and catchers of South Africa and South America, you must always keep the snake's head away from you at all times.


Trapping a Snake

Sometimes, in order to effectively triumph over a snake you have to expose them to the wider population. Engaging a snake in a "one-on-one" battle is not only dangerous, but also ineffective.

In the wild, simply cutting a snake's head off in a direct attack does not remove the danger completely but merely reduces it.

It is better to catch a snake alive and redeploy them to another area as an example to other snakes in the office. The most effective way to trap one is to first lure it out of its hiding place; this is done by lowering the temperature of its environment, because snakes, being cold-blooded, need to regulate their body temperature to survive, so they can be effectively lured out of hiding when there is a sudden drop in their core temperature. They will always leave their hiding place to look for a warmer area. Once exposed, you must use a stick or pole to distract the snake's head and then lift it by the tail and place it into a sack or pillowcase, ensuring that the bag is sufficiently strong to avoid protrusions from the snake's poisonous fangs.

Catching a corporate snake is no different, in that you must take the heat out of the toxic interaction by not rising to their behavior and always showing restraint. This will upset the snake, and it will always seek a more heated encounter, but this will now attract the attention of others in the office.

You are essentially baiting the snake into a situation where their aggression and behavior will be exposed. Once exposed, they are completely distracted, and you are also seen to take the high road by not engaging with the head as you quickly dispose of them.

## *Lizards* (Squamata)

Office lizards are in abundance in all corporations. They are determined creatures who always appear to be in a hurry, scurrying around the office carrying out tasks that seem superfluous and self-serving. Although they appear harmless, office lizards are extremely deadly to rivals and other species owing to their underhanded behavior.

Their unassuming stature allows them to permeate most crevices in order to obtain information that will be used to their own betterment. They are known for spreading rumors and, being cold-blooded, bask in heated environments.

Lizards appear to have a shiny and smooth appearance, so they will always be recognizable in new suits and dresses, but in reality, this is misleading as their skin is dry like that of all other reptiles.

### High Profile Lizard: Malaysian Water Monitor (*Varanus salvator*)

Native to Borneo and Sumatran rain forests, these fearsome predators, averaging around 8 feet in length and weighing up to 30 kg, are a formidable adversary. They have a large arsenal at their disposal, such as sharp claws, teeth, and powerful tails as weapons in their onslaught. They are also highly venomous.

### Dealing with a Lizard

Interacting with lizards is a fickle affair. With the exception of monitors, they are normally quite a small species (in the physical sense) and can wangle their way into most situations but mainly thrive in heated situations where conflict is present. They are self-serving and duplicitous and spread office gossip, so they should be not be trusted or confided in. They will also seek to take credit for ideas and achievements that are not their own. You should, however, sporadically feed them misinformation that will be used to your advantage.

As they carry messages to and from multiple departments, you can strategically control this flow of information by how much and what you tell a lizard. For example, leaking information of a fictitious departmental audit can see rises in productivity.

## Trapping a Lizard

When a lizard enters your environment there are a few solutions that can successfully remove them, one of the most effective being the use of cold water.

As lizards are cold-blooded and constantly need to regulate their temperature, a spray with cold water will dramatically lower their core temperature and stop them immediately in their tracks. Once immobilized, they can be covered by a box and relocated.

The same logic applies when dealing with corporate lizards also; you must stop them dead in their tracks by shocking them with cold water, this being facts. Situations can be orchestrated whereby they can be exposed, as when delivering incorrect information (disinformation created by you) to senior managers. Once they have been exposed as duplicitous gossipers, their reputations are destroyed, and they will shrink back into the shadows again.

## *Turtles and Tortoises* (Testudines)

Turtles are the oldest living reptiles on the planet and have remained more or less unchanged over the last 200 million years. Scientists attribute this longevity to their shell, a natural armor that can allow them to be completely protected from predators. Therefore, they have no need to change or adapt; they are safe. This is true in the workplace also, where office turtles refuse to change their ways and will continue to do things in the way that works best for them. Turtles are seen as a source of wisdom owing to their longevity, but this can also be a problem for coworkers and managers because they refuse to adapt to new ways of working or innovative approaches to activities. Turtles are also not social creatures; far from being team players, they insist on working alone because they believe they "know best." However, they have a wealth of intimate and technical knowledge that can keep organizations afloat and are therefore valued by senior managers even though they can be extremely frustrated by their behaviors.

## Tortoises

All tortoises are turtles, but not all turtles are tortoises. The main difference between the two is that turtles spend most of their lives either in or near water, whereas tortoises are almost exclusively land dwellers.

## High Profile Turtle: Mata Mata Turtle (Chelus fimbriata)

This unusual creature, indigenous to the Amazon basin, can reach lengths of up to 45 cm and can weigh up to 20 kg. "Mata" Mata," which translates as "kill-kill" in Spanish, characteristically sit motionless in shallow waters and use their large mouths in a vacuum like process to suck in prey. They are, however, often stepped on accidentally by humans and deliver extremely nasty bites that can lead to severed toes.

## Dealing with a Turtle

Interacting with a turtle can be a frustrating affair. You are essentially dealing with a person who is the most experienced in the organization but not necessarily the most talented. (Some are both, however, and so can be equally as frustrating.) Corporate turtles will always have only one way of doing things—their way—so you must take on board what they have to say and what they offer to the situation at hand. They must be respected for their services and long tenure and will get aggressive if they perceive any ounce of disrespect or condemnation. They have a nasty bite, so expect to be put in your place quite quickly if you cross them.

When they feel threatened, they can also "work to rule," further slowing down operations, so in order to successfully interact with corporate turtles you must show real patience and respect. Playing to their egos will not work, because office turtles have been around a long time and will recognize this tactic immediately as being insincere. Turtles take great pride in their work and will always seek to leave a lasting legacy.

## Trapping a Turtle

I have no idea why anyone would want to trap or expose a turtle; it will not do you any harm unless it feels threatened. Nevertheless, there may be situations where action is called for, so I will not be accused of species discrimination.

To expose a turtle, you are essentially challenging their entire existence. They live and breathe their work and take great pride when they are called upon to solve problems or provide expert guidance. It makes them feel needed in an ever-changing world dominated by technological advances.

So this is how they can be trapped…Turtles are, essentially, "neo-Luddites," who are opposed to technological advances or radical change within the workplace because they feel threatened.

Turtles have egos, so to be upstaged by technology lowers their morale. In order to effectively trap a turtle, therefore, you must overwhelm them with innovation and technology. They will refuse to cooperate, not out of ability but out of ego and sheer stubbornness. They will then be seen as blockers and sidelined by senior management.

## Crocodiles, Alligators, and Caimans (Crocodilians)

The only jungle member of the Crocodilians are caimans. These are formidable creatures that can grow between 5 and 20 feet in length and weigh up to 1,000 lbs (as heavy as a grand piano). These fearsome predators have

a powerful and imposing presence, have a thick skin, and possess an excellent sense of hearing and sight. They see and know all that goes on within a department and even sleep with one eye open.

Office caimans are solitary creatures, however, and do not like gathering with peers, doing so only when absolutely necessary as during team meetings and briefings, and even then, they keep themselves to themselves.

Caimans are top jungle predators and are hunted only by large anaconda snakes and jaguars, their position near the top of the food chain dictating their demeanor. Owing to their cold-blooded makeup, they spend their days basking in the sun and regulating their temperature so it can appear that they do not do a lot of actual work. The fear that they instill in others drives others to work hard in case of reprisals. They are masters of attrition and can last months without food.

Despite being extremely intimidating in office environments, they are revered by direct peers in high positions because their work performance has a positive impact on other teams, giving them the image of highly intelligent and unassailable allies to have. Caimans are normally found in senior management or director roles.

High Profile Black Caiman (*Melanosuchus niger*)

This aggressive apex predator, native to the Amazon basin can grow up to 20 feet and can weigh up to 500 kg. Its fearsome jaws are designed to catch a multitude of prey and can snap shut with over 4,000 lbs of pressure per square inch.

Dealing with a Caiman

Interacting with a caiman is not pleasant. They are apex predators and will not hesitate to destroy you on sight. They will also take great delight in doing so.

They will snatch you from the sidelines with their large powerful jaws and then take you on a "death roll" to the bottom of the river in order to drown you. Once drowned, they will then swallow you whole.

They not only kill you, but really go to town on you. The trick in interacting with a corporate caiman is not to upset them at all; this may sound much too obvious to deserve mention, but never has it been so true.

Do not interrupt or challenge them, and always allow them to feel in control of the situation. Caimans must feel that they have your instant respect. They do not take compliments well and will often attack when you use these tactics on them. They expect the utmost respect but do not show fear, because to be fearful in the presence of a caiman is to invite trouble, they are quick to pick up on this and question your motives. To give a caiman respect shows the caiman that you too are able to recognize its achievements and therefore hold the same values.

Trapping a Caiman

Trapping a caiman can be a suicide mission, but sometimes desperate times can call for desperate measures. As mentioned earlier, their powerful jaws can snap shut with over 4,000 lbs of pressure per square inch, but, consequently, these powerful jaws have very little opening strength and can normally be held shut very easily by rubber bands. It is therefore recommended that in all attempts to trap a caiman you must concentrate on the mouth. Removing its ability to use its powerful jaws effectively renders it helpless.

This is the same in the corporate environment, where you must reduce their ability to bite.

One unorthodox method when attempting to trap caimans is to observe their movements and establish when they have eaten. Once a large meal is consumed whole, a caiman is essentially weighed down by the weight of its meal, so it will lower its reactionary movements, making it less susceptible to hearing and defending an ambush. Corporate caimans are no different, because after they have destroyed a victim, they are less likely to go back on the hunt for quite some time. This is the opportunity to pounce and secure the jaws with rubber bands. Owing to their slow metabolism, a meal may not occur that often, so you must lie in wait. After a kill, corporate caimans are suspicious of all around them and are at their most vulnerable, wishing to understand how their actions were perceived by others, and overanalyzing whether it has given them more respect or whether they have they gone too far this time. And for a small window in time they fear reprisal from HR and their peers in higher positions. This is when you approach a caiman and get what you want from the situation.

This vulnerability and lack of self-confidence is short-lived, however, as their natural aggression and arrogance kick back in, and they return to themselves.

## Birds

Birds are another diverse group of creatures found in the workplace. Approximately two-thirds of all birdlife are found in rain forests. Birds have one distinct advantage over all other creatures in the rain forest (except insects), namely, their ability to fly. Having the gift of flight in the office is also no different in that it gives office birds an advantage over their flightless coworkers. Most office birds are practically untouchable, cannot be easily caught, and are faster and quicker than everyone else, given their ability to escape danger very easily. Despite these enviable attributes, some office birds lack self-awareness and are extremely self-involved. They are easily startled, and it takes them some time to gain your trust. In view of their omni presence and effective maneuverability, office birds are normally found in roles where they are required to partner other parts of the business, usually providing communication services. They span multiple social circles and easily move from one to the other. Most birds are extremely social creatures and can be found in large flocks and are easily recognized by loud distinctive sounds and calls. They are excellent providers of updates on organizational change and even office gossip.

Corporate birds can be grouped into five subcategories:

1. **Parrots** (*Psittaciformes*)
2. **Songbirds** (*Passeriformes*)
3. **Pheasants, Chickens, Peacocks, and Turkeys** (*Galliformess*)
4. **Falcons** (*Falconiformes*)
5. **Eagles and Vultures** (*Accipitriformes*)

## Parrots (Psittaciformes)

These brightly colored, gregarious, and fashionably dressed birds are usually heard in the office before they are seen. Needing constant attention from others, parrots are highly social creatures within the workplace and like to display themselves in a confident and "vibrant" manner.

Macaws are the largest of the parrot species (All macaws are parrots but not vice versa) and are viewed as one of the most intelligent species of birds in the world. This portrayal often adds a lot of pressure to office parrots hoping to live up to everyone's expectations and perform well in all tasks. Owing to their high levels of intelligence, macaws find themselves exposed to many corporate practices that they do not agree with and sometimes have to put profit before people or turn a blind eye to corruption. This makes them feel uneasy. The flamboyance displayed by the parrot is unnatural, being merely a method of concealing insecurities in which office parrots spend a lot of time pretending to be someone that they do not want to be. This weighs the office parrots down with negativity and sometimes guilt, and, exactly as in the wild, in order to survive the effects of toxins in their diet, parrots must consume clay to neutralize these effects. The clay is considered something outside of normal office characteristic behavior such as returning to their roots before they truly lose themselves in their acts.

High Profile: Hyacinth Macaw (*Anodorhynchus hyacinthinus*)

Native to the South American tropics, the hyacinth macaw is the largest of all parrot species. From head to tail tip it can exceed lengths of over 3 feet and can weigh in excess of 2 kg. A highly intelligent bird, the hyacinth macaw can even use tools to help when eating.

Dealing with a Parrot

Dealing with a parrot can be quite daunting because it belongs to one of the most intelligent bird species and possesses an array of talents and skills unique to most birds. So when combined with its glitzy flamboyant demeanor, it can intimidate even the most confident of animals.

Parrots, as a result of their high achievements, have limited patience when dealing with others. They want information fast and accurately and will normally operate on a level of productivity exceeding that of many other staff in the office. When interacting with a parrot try and mirror its enthusiasm and agility; you need to be quick and confident in your actions in order to gain its respect. A parrot will size you up on the first interaction and always keep this opinion; so the phrase "you only have one shot at a first impression" rings very true in this situation. Getting on the wrong side of a parrot can have a negative effect on your corporate brand, given the respect it commands and receive within all organizations; being underrated by a parrot can impede your career advancements.

Trapping a Parrot

Parrots, despite their intelligence and abilities, can be a real nuisance to be around with. They can use their status and reputational abilities to embarrass other species and can detract from team project goals by not focusing on the bland but vital core issues but rather seeking to partake in tasks that will garner them praise and admiration. Projects can therefore suffer on account of its relentless selfish pursuit of admiration.

In these instances, the only recourse is to make the parrot lose interest. This is done in many ways, but, essentially, all point to the strategy that you simply must bore them with information.

Corporate parrots will thrive only in action-packed dramatic situations but lose interest in mundane activities because they are not platforms for them to shine. You must seek to blind the parrot from activities that result in praise and gratitude. When a wild parrot cannot see the sun properly and suddenly finds itself in increased darkness, its natural reaction is to freeze. Once frozen it is, essentially, exposed to all members of the team.

### Songbirds: (Passennes)

Songbirds, by their very name, are extremely vocal and possess one of the most developed vocal organs of all bird species. They are usually passive by nature but can sometimes fall prey to their own egos and take on "diva"-like personalities akin to those displayed by their office counterparts.

When you hear a songbird singing it is usually a male using his song to mark his territory or to attract a mate. These songs therefore serve a purpose and are not merely indicators or expressions of joy, so don't be fooled by these faux displays of happiness.

Songbirds possess a highly developed flexor tendon that allows them to lock their feet in place as they sing, so they have adapted to carrying out this performance quite well. Similarly, their office counterparts will usually find a perch to strategically locate themselves in order to be heard better by all around them. Their song is usually a carefully rehearsed rant sung in order to get them noticed or mark out their own office territories.

One point to note, however, is that songbirds are not born with the innate ability to sing their family's songs, and these must be learned from other birds in the family, so there is always someone behind the scenes either encouraging or misleading office songbirds either directly or indirectly.

## High Profile: Vogelkop Superb Bird-of-Paradise (*Lophorina niedda*)

Native to the tropics of New Guinea, these remarkable birds are a sight to behold. Their elaborate displays of courtship involve energetic exhibitions of song and dance. To set the scene for this exhibition, the male birds tidy up their environment, ensuring that it is spotless before females arrive.

## Dealing with a Songbird

Interacting with a songbird can be a weary task. The endless moaning and pontificating can wear down even the most resilient of people. To get what you want from the situation, you must simply listen to them and be seen to be in agreement with their complaints. Faux empathy and sympathy can be used to gain their trust and ensure that they provide you with the information you require.

## Trapping a Songbird

Songbirds can, however, be quite dangerous if their moaning and pontificating is directed toward you. It can have an effect on your reputation and cause unnecessary annoyance or stress. To combat this, you must seek to call its bluff. Publicly challenge them to provide better ideas and solutions rather than just moan at you. You must then seek to orchestrate situations where they are "left holding the baby."

An Ocelot is a trap used in the wild that traps a bird's feet when it lands on a carefully constructed device resembling a perch. The same method can be used on corporate songbirds, and so when they get up on their soapbox to have a rant, they will find themselves stuck (essentially holding the responsibility for an issue) and will be exposed to all.

### Pheasants, Peacocks, Chickens, and Turkeys (Galliformes)

Office Galliformes are the least versatile of the office bird species and are usually unable to perform at the appropriate level required by their role. These ground-dwelling foragers lack the abilities and talents of other bird species but "talk a good game."

Contrary to popular belief, however, they can fly but only in short bursts, never higher than a few feet and only for a short distance. This awkward display of "flight" is usually preceded by an elaborate garish takeoff. Not being able to fly as well as other office birds, they attempt to cover up this fact and pretend that they can; they are notorious bluffers, often convincing others that they have skills far beyond their actual capabilities.

Office Galliformes are slow and unable to keep up with the pace required to succeed in many tasks. They lack the integrity to defend their team or colleagues or even themselves when attacked. This is similar to their behavior in the wild, where they do not instinctively defend their territory when attacked or threatened. They lack conviction but possess a strong sense of self-praise, vanity, and arrogance, which is used to mask their shortcomings from being exposed. They mark their territory by strutting around, flapping their wings, and ruffling their feathers in an attempt to establish dominance, but when ultimately challenged will normally run away.

Galliformes are usually from privileged backgrounds but despite having attended a privileged school they did not excel there and now just rely on associations with prestigious institutions or people as their only achievement.

## Dealing with Galliformes

Dealing with the office galliform is a painful experience. Arrogance and self-riotousness will be displayed at every turn, but you must understand that these are attempts to cover up their inabilities, and they will lead you around in circles rather than give you straight answers. They will constantly remind you of who they are and how in their opinion the organization could not function without them. You must play the game with galliformes, because attacking them outright will result in a huge commotion and restraint must therefore be adopted at all times. To survive an encounter successfully, you will need to play to their egos in order to get any sort of movement. Galliformes will always have a second-in-command that actually does all their work for them, so this person will be mentioned in all conversations, and you will now have a person to approach to actually get the information that you require.

## Trapping Galliformes

Galliformes are one of the easiest groups of birds to catch. Their lack of flight makes them easy targets, and their pride always blinds their common sense, making them easy to bait and very easily led. Wild galliformes are baited with seeds and nuts, and the office environment is no different. Strategically placed lures can attract the galliform and maneuver them to wherever you wish them to go. They are attracted by anything that massages their ego, makes them look good, or gains them praise, so bear this in mind when creating effective bait.

## High Profile: Green Peacock (*Pavo muticus*)

Native to the rain forests of Southeast Asia, the Green Peacock is the largest of all galliformes, reaching seven feet in length (including feather train) and weighing up to 4 kg. Its flashy feathers are designed for display purposes only in attracting a mate.

## Birds of Prey

Rain forest birds of prey include the Accipitriformes (eagles, hawks, and vultures) and the Falconiformes (Falcons), which dominate all rain forest environments as apex avian predators.

Like their office counterparts, birds of prey live high up on the emergent layer and do not have many natural predators (some have none). Similar to the directors on the board of corporate entities, they are almost untouchable.

### Falcons (Falconiformes)

These fearsome hunters have eyesight more than eight times more effective than that of many other birds and possess excellent hearing, making it nearly impossible to hide from them. They can dive toward prey at speeds of over 240 mph and can catch prey from any environment, aquatic or land based. They screech to alert all within hearing range of their power and to mark their territory. They are the people whom you have to approach cap in hand for approval of a budget or permission for a project to commence. They have keen attention to detail, and nothing gets past them.

Office falcons are on top of their game and yield huge power in all organisations but have one natural foe that is more dominant and larger… the corporate eagle.

## High Profile: Peregrine Falcon (*Falco Peregrinus*)

This avian predator, native to Central America, is the fastest animal on the planet. It has been known to have attained speeds of over 240 mph in snatching its prey in midair.

## Dealing with a Falcon

Falcons are masters of authority in any organization, so dealing with them, unless you outrank them, is actually very straightforward: Essentially, you must listen and do what they say—as simple as that.

It will outmaneuver you at every turn and should not be challenged without good reason. Challenging a falcon can also be career suicide, so you must learn to bite your tongue when dealing with them. If you have an issue you must appear measured and communicate respectfully and concisely, removing emotion from every interaction. Corporate falcons do not beat about the bush and will always be direct and to the point; they will expect the same in return.

## Trapping a Falcon

You are entering very dangerous territory in an attempt to trap or expose a corporate falcon. The only way to catch or trap a falcon (and indeed all birds of prey) is to use live bait.

In view of the extreme speeds that falcons can achieve; a "Dho Gaza" trap is the most effective way to catch falcons in the wild and catching corporate falcons is no different. Essentially, a falcon swoops down to catch prey baited in front of a large net. Once the bird catches the prey it hits the net, which closes around them trapping them in place. The speed and predatory nature of the falcon is, essentially, used against them.

The prey selected for this task will be situation specific, and the net will normally be a sting that exposes financial or governance mismanagement.

### Eagles and Vultures (Accipitriformes)

### Eagles

Eagles sit at the top of the avian food chain; they have zero avian predators and are, essentially, hunting machines. They are symbols of power and freedom in many cultures and are the largest birds of prey in any office environment. They can spot prey over 2 miles away, their eyes being pitched at 30 degrees from the center of their face to enhance their field of vision. They see everything, missing nothing. They can see more colors than humans and can even see in ultraviolet, essentially being able to see things that you cannot.

Being innate hunting machines, eagle chicks even take advantage of their weaker siblings by taking their food. These chicks normally die, with the strongest chick declared the winner of this morbid kindergarten game, a game of "survival of the fittest," which the parents not only watch with interest but also encourage. Office eagles can therefore come from environments where they are pushed or groomed for success by pushy parents or even possibly possess this drive just to please their parents. Office eagles are proud creatures with a strong sense of entitlement. They make decisions with conviction and confidence and even in the wild are the only birds not to look over their shoulder for predators before they dive, as they have no avian predators.

High Profile: Harpy Eagle (*Harpia harpyja*)

This native Central American bird of prey is the largest eagle in the world, weighing over 4 kg and having a wingspan of over 7 feet. Living on the emergent layer of the rain forest, they have no natural predators. Having the largest talons of any other eagle allows them to swoop down and snatch many species more easily than any other bird of prey.

## Dealing with an Eagle

Interactions with an eagle are similar to those with corporate falcons, described earlier, but only on a much larger scale. Eagles are one of the most feared and respected species within any organization, and interactions always go one way—theirs.

Professional courtesy and respect are essential attributes when dealing with a corporate eagle no matter what the circumstance because you are normally dealing with the leader of the organization.

## Trapping an Eagle

If you do have a death wish and need to expose or trap a corporate eagle, you must be willing to accept the consequences. These interactions normally include whistleblower legislation, and you must be sure and confident that you really wish to pursue this route. This is, essentially, a coup d'état, and you must realize that as soon as you engage in this process it will become bigger than you could have ever imagined and that the fallout will be insurmountable. This is said not to discourage you from following your convictions but to make you aware of the gravity of trapping a corporate eagle, an undertaking that will normally include some level of political, legal, or law enforcement involvement at some point in the proceedings.

## Vultures

This species of corporate bird differs greatly from the hawks and eagles described earlier. Vultures are the only birds of prey that do not personally kill their prey. They are carrion eaters, surviving off dead animals. They

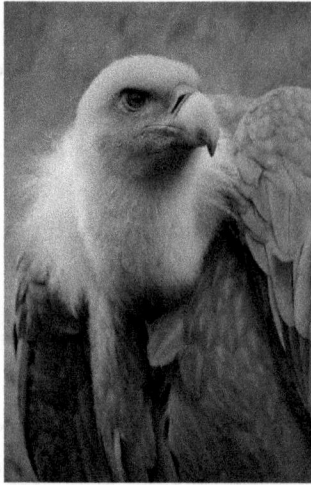

are referred to as "nature's clean-up crew" because they get rid of dead bodies by eating virtually every part of an animal, including the bones. Strong acids in their stomach break down the bones and absorb them entirely, leaving no trace of their existence. This practice minimizes infection and diseases from the dead animals and reduces the impact on the wider environment. Corporate vultures are no different, making problems go away and using their intelligence to deflect unwanted attention. I'm not suggesting that things are done illegally; the intention is to ensure that things are taken care of before they create a scene or have a negative impact on the organization. Vultures fly higher than any other species of birds and normally use this to the company's advantage when dealing with complex sensitive issues because they can see the whole picture better than everyone else.

Vultures excel in executing a clever spin whenever one is required to turn any issue into something positive.

### High Profile: King Vulture (Sarcoramphus papa)

Weighing up to 6 kg and having a wingspan of up to seven feet makes the King Vulture the largest vulture in Central America. Their name derives from ancient observation (still apparent today) of how all other vultures would move out of the way and let the king have the first dips on any carrion prey when he arrived on the scene.

Dealing with a Vulture

Vultures are extremely menacing creatures; they appear only when an animal is either dying or dead, have no guilty conscience because they didn't personally contribute to the kill and therefore possess unusually warped interpretations of ethics. When they are interacting with you it is usually in the capacity of a messenger of death. They are deeply profound and philosophical creatures but use carefully selected dogmatic knowledge as justification to support their distorted sense of morality. When dealing with a corporate vulture you should only deal in facts and not try and justify your motivations, because these will not be taken on board. All emotion must be removed, and you must always remain calm and collected in their presence. You should never show any weakness in front of a vulture and always portray a position of courage and conviction.

Trapping a Vulture

When trying to trap or expose a vulture you must play to their natural genetic predispositions.

They are designed to seek out and eat dead or dying animals, and that is exactly the perfect lure.

Feigning an injury or problematic matter will attract these birds when they feel that you are in a downfall, and when they approach the "prey," that is when you reveal the charade.

Everyone understands that vultures go after vulnerable prey, but this exposure of vultures hunting strong and able workers will concern the office and alert everyone to its antics, and, as a consequence, the vulture will not approach you again.

# Creepy Crawlies

The most abundant category of life in all rain forests, creepy crawlies are also present in workplaces. Despite being seen as either pests or food by many other species, they do serve a purpose and can rise through the ranks in many organizations by their stealth and unassuming demeanor. They can also be extremely dangerous.

The group is too diverse to provide collective information on common attributes and behaviors, so each species must be individually studied.

Broadly, Office "Creepy Crawlies" can be broken down into two groups and eight distinct subgroups

Arthropods
1. **Spiders, Scorpions** (*Arachnids*)
2. **Centipedes, Millipedes** (*Myriapods*)
3. **Ants** (*Formicidae*)
4. **Bees** (*Apoidea*)
5. **Wasps and Hornets** (*Vespa*)
6. **Mosquitos and Flies** (Diptera)
7. **Butterflies and Moths (including Caterpillars)** (*Lepidoptera*)

Molluscs
8. **Snails and Slugs** (*Gastropods*)

### Spiders, Scorpions (Arachnids)

Arachnids are in abundance in corporate environments. The old phrase "you're never more than ten feet away from a spider" is very fitting. Spiders are extremely beneficial in ecosystems as they catch and eat more pests than many other creatures.

### Spiders

Spiders don't have bones but have hard exoskeletons used as armor that they molt regularly in order to grow. Wild spiders remain hidden and set

traps for their victims, and office spiders are no different. They are masters of catching vulnerable colleagues with the use of strategic trapping techniques. By examining the quality and design of spider webs in the wild, scientists can detect air pollutants and chemicals in the environment. Analogously, in the corporate world senior management condone the use of these traps because they are an effective way of gauging corporate practice regarding corruption and compliance. Having webs as deterrents keeps workers on the straight and narrow. Spiders are also some of the most venomous creatures on earth, and their bite can be fatal.

High Profile: Brazilian Wandering Spider *Phoneutria fera*

This eight-legged assassin with a leg span of over 15 cm wanders the rain forest floors at night hunting its prey. Having a Latin name meaning "murderesses," it is the most venomous species of spider on earth and its bite can lead to severe respiratory and cardiac problems and lead to death.

Dealing with a Spider

A corporate spider will always try to catch you out. Entrapment will always be their goal in stressful situations in attempts to draw attention away from themselves. So in any dealings with a spider, you must carefully record all interactions. Minutes and notes must be taken of all exchanges, and, wherever possible, have witnesses present at meetings.

Trapping a Spider

Spiders are invertebrates but have a tough exoskeleton that is used as armor but is quite restrictive; so in order to grow, spiders in the wild must shed this exoskeleton in a process known as molting. When they shed their exoskeleton they are, essentially, completely vulnerable to predators because they have no defenses. This is applicable in the corporate world also, in that corporate spiders wishing to advance in their careers must take stock of all the deeds that they are currently involved in to ensure that they have left no loose ends. This period of reflection, usually before an interview or potential promotional advancement, is when the spider is at its most vulnerable and will not be in attack mode because it is consumed with the prospect of being promoted. This is where you strike and expose their wrongdoings.

### Scorpions

Scorpions are masters of attrition and can survive in almost any environment. They are fast and extremely venomous to both predators and prey. They use large pincers to grab prey and then follow up with a sting from the tail to render the helpless victims immobile. They also possess a hard exoskeleton, used as armor, and are expert hunters. Office scorpions are no different; they are feared in their department as being extremely sharp and cutting, they lack basic social skills and pleasantries and will attack you if deemed a threat. Conversations initiated by corporate scorpions are concise and to the point, aimed at extracting whatever information is necessary.

High Profile: Brazilian Yellow Scorpion (*Tityus serrulatus*)

This tiny South American arachnid, reaching sizes of no more than 7 cm, is the most venomous scorpion species in South America, causing hundreds of human deaths and thousands of casualties each year. In addition to pulmonary and respiratory issues, its bite causes paralysis and neurological complications.

Dealing with a Scorpion

Interactions with a corporate scorpion are not pleasant. You both know that they can cause you serious harm. They are notorious for damaging reputations of many corporate animals by inflicting serious pain that can have long-lasting psychological repercussions. When in the presence of a scorpion, do not upset it and always draw the conversation back to a place of calmness and structure. It will constantly look for ways to attack you if it senses any vulnerability, so always appear strong in its presence.

## Trapping a Scorpion

Corporate scorpions, despite having a fearsome reputation as with all bullies, do not like attention. They dislike their actions being viewed publicly by others and prefer to do their evil bidding in private in order to create better psychological effects for their victims.

Once exposed, however, a corporate scorpion will retreat out of public view immediately. In the wild all scorpions glow under ultraviolet light. No one is really certain why they do this, but it is thought that they do this to highlight to themselves their level of exposure so they can retreat to a safe position and avoid being revealed. This is how you effectively deal with corporate scorpions too; you simply need to expose their activities to other people. This will reduce their power and they will retreat. As with any bully, when their behavior is exposed to others, they normally do not like it and cease.

### Centipedes, Millipedes (Myriapods)

In the wild, Myriapods are critical in the processes of recycling dead plants and other organic material. Corporate myriapods are often overlooked in many organizations owing to their size and selfless behavior. Despite being rarely seen, they too play a vital role in organizational upkeep.

Millipedes are the more impactful than centipedes in their day-to-day operations because they feast solely on plants, and in the corporate world, they keep the office floors and departments operating.

They meticulously tidy, sort, file, and maintain equipment and infrastructure to ensure day-to-day core operations flow smoothly.

Centipedes are normally larger and faster, however, and are also carnivorous. These attributes also make them efficient in their organizational skills in that they ensure that the environments are correctly policed and managed so that core operations can function.

Myriapods therefore normally excel in roles that require extremely strong organizational skills.

## High Profile: Amazonian Giant Centipede (*Scolopendra gigantean*)

Reaching lengths of up to 30 cm, this Central American predator is the largest species of centipede in the world. It possesses a potent venom in its bite that can be extremely painful which can lead to death.

## Dealing with a Centipede

Interacting with a centipede can leave you feeling drained as they are constantly on the move trying to organize and manage tasks to the point of exhaustion. The best way of tolerating these creatures is to simply let them organize the task at hand and let them move on. They will not dwell too much on any single issue, so it's best to give them what they want and let them be on their way.

## Trapping a Centipede

When it is deemed necessary, however, to trap or expose a corporate centipede, the really only effective way to do this is to take away their ability to move. This is identical in the wild, where centipedes are really only successfully immobilized when their environment becomes too dry so they will as a result, always seek out a source of rehydration. As primitive or as obvious as it sounds, it is actually the most useful way to stop a corporate centipede in its tracks. They are usually stopped when you constantly keep moving the goalposts of their tasks; they will not like this, because they need to see completion in their endeavors and will simply be too overwhelmed and demotivated when no clear end of their project can be seen or achieved, so they will completely cease work.

## Ants (Formicidea)

Ants are the most intelligent species of insects, possessing 250,000 brain cells. A colony of 40,000 ants have the same intelligence of that of a human being. Their colonies are a microcosm of the utopian corporate culture sought after by many senior leaders within every organization. They have a form of cooperation and team working ability unmatched by any species in the living world. The hierarchy within the colony is normally structured into three categories of ant: The queen, the female workers, and the males (whose only job is to mate)

This teamwork and loyalty displayed by office ants is so refined and productive that ants function as a superorganism, with each team member contributing to the overall performance of the team and putting the team's needs before its own individual requirements.

Office Ants are similar insofar as they have loyalty to their high-performing teams and contribute to overall organizational success. Issues arise, however, when Ant Queens at department head level are held in higher regard than senior directors, and there is always politics at play. Ants are driven, meticulous, and extremely resilient, being able to carry up to 30 times their own body weight.

Ants can go to war with other colonies, and this is promoted by senior leaders as a way of instilling competition necessary for corporate productivity levels to remain high. Ants, being the determined creatures that they are, will normally fight to the death, so the herd can be culled in these competitive interactions. Ants are unique in that they can also take prisoners and force them to work for them after they raid their colony, similar to the situation that can arise when departments merge.

## High Profile: Bullet Ant (*Paraponera clavata*)

This tiny South American predator has a nasty reputation, with its name linked to the effect of the pain experienced from a bullet wound after being shot. It has the most painful sting of any ant species, and its effects normally last 24 hours. The pain is so severe that it causes the victims to sweat profusely and drift in and out of consciousness while simultaneously the victim's heart and breathing rates can be dangerously elevated and can in some cases lead to death.

## Dealing with an Ant

Interaction with an ant can either be extremely positive or extremely frustrating depending on the specific task at hand. Ants are single-track-minded and can carry out only one objective but with such skilled precision that it is a joy to behold.

If your activities are aligned with those of the ant, then it will be a relatively effortless encounter because you will get exactly what you are looking for and more; however, if what you are looking for goes against the ant's natural instincts or abilities, your encounter will not be so rewarding.

The important point to note when dealing with all ants is that you must be aware of the ant's skills and limitations and not pursue a request that is out of its control, because you will only be frustrated. When dealing with an ant you also must remember that you are never just dealing with one ant but with a colony and a part of a greater whole.

## Trapping an Ant

As mentioned earlier, dealing with an ant means, essentially, dealing with the ethos of the wider colony because they are deemed creatures with innate loyalty to their colony and queen. To really trap or expose a colony of ants, you must go after the queen, because once a queen dies or is displaced, the colony collapses.

In the wild, an ant queen can sometimes produce fewer eggs in order to conserve her energy to counter any rivalries that may take place from other potential queens, essentially ensuring her survival on the throne. When this fact of the queen putting herself before the colony is revealed to the ants, they will form a rebellion and overthrow the queen, which will lead to the colony's ultimate demise. To effectively do this in the corporate world, you must play to the queen's insecurities and encourage her to look after herself. You must remember that in order for the clique to have been formed in the first place, something must have upset the queen: She was either overlooked for a promotion or is unhappy with certain aspects of the corporate culture and so has designed her own ecosystem operating in parallel to the wider organization's goals. Once reminded of these motivations, the queen's ego will kick in, and she will start carrying out self-edifying tasks that will set off alarm bells in her workforce. You are essentially destabilizing a corporate clique.

## Bees (Apoidea)

Bees are remarkable creatures within any corporate environment. Unlike other colony species, the output that bees produce (honey) is the only insect foodstuff suitable for human consumption. Corporate Bees are therefore exploited by all corporations as being of great economic importance, with the fruits of their labor being used and controlled by others. Bees' honey production is responsible for over a third of all the food that we eat owing to their activities of pollination. Bees are therefore vital to all life, and the corporate world is no different. The knock-on effect from the economic output of bees allows other corporate entities to keep afloat and survive. Without corporate bees, organizations will fail. Bees do not sleep but remain motionless to conserve energy for the next day's activities; they are relentless in their pursuit of success.

Bees have a very short life cycle and die after only 6 weeks. Corporate Bees can be found on many trading or sales floors making vast amount of money for organizations and retiring quite young. Bees are, however, not born with the knowledge of how to make honey; it is a skill that they must learn from other "older" bees within the colony. In the corporate world it is a very select and intense internship, with positions for "corporate bee" type roles requiring extensive training and suited only to highly talented specific individuals. As with other colony species (ants), issues arise when queen bees at department head level are held in higher regard than senior directors and there is always politics at play.

Unlike ant colonies, removing a queen bee will not lead to the colony collapse. When the queen is removed a new queen is selected by the workers from the larva and fed "royal jelly," essentially anointing her into the new position to carry on the activities of the hive.

Bees have excellent memories and attention to detail; they can recognize human faces and are being studied by scientists in relation to advancements in human facial recognition software.

## High Profile: African Honeybee—(*Apis mellifera*) Hybrid

This species, often referred to as "Killer bees" are actually a hybrid invasive species that now inhabit South America, having escaped from a research facility in the 1950s. These aggressive insects have killed thousands of humans and can chase victims for over a mile.

## Dealing with a Bee

Being colony creatures, interactions with corporate bees are quite similar to interactions with corporate ants, the main difference being that bees are corporate capitalists and ants are more socialist creatures. Everything that bees do have a commercial focus, and they will not care about any other aspect of a project's life cycle. They are motivated by money and can sometimes be blinded by this fact, so the best way to fully engage a bee is to speak its language; you must highlight to them the specific benefit of carrying out a task and always try and link it back to savings or revenue and how it can be useful in these endeavors. Only then will it fully engage in the process.

Trapping a Bee

Unlike trapping corporate ants, corporate bees are not beaten once the queen is killed or displaced.

Your only option here is to seek to replace the queen bee with another, more manageable one.

This is fraught with danger, however, because displacing a corporate bee (in view of the positive effects that the colony has on all organizational growth) will incur the wrath not only of the colony but also of the entire organization; so you must proceed with great caution. You will also not be completely sure that the new successor will adhere to your way of thinking, because the power of their new position may go to their head.

Queen bees are also no easy targets: They are not only fiercely protected by the colony, but are also deadly creatures to interact with, because, unlike the single stinging capabilities of her workers, queen bees can repeatedly sting a victim.

Queen bees are also threatened by other potential queens and will instinctively seek out and kill any perceived rivals even at the larval stage. A queen bee therefore prefers docile and subservient female workers that are loyal to her and views any individual success as an attempt to upstage her. The queen bee must take credit for all success achieved by the colony. One way to expose a queen bee is to give one or all of her worker bees public praise for their efforts; continual praise of her workers by others will make the queen nervous because you are, essentially, attributing the achievement gained to the workers and not the queen; if this happens repeatedly she will be trapped because she cannot publicly dismiss the successful worker and must grit her teeth and put up with this process. If this happens on a regular basis, the queen bee will be furious and act aggressively to all around her. This aggression will lead to her downfall because she will become less productive and her colony will turn on her and ultimately replace her. This is where you use your influence or assist in their selection.

### Wasps and Hornets (Vespa)

Members of this species are the poor cousins of bees and are constantly reminded of these shortcomings, a fact that makes them highly aggressive, uncooperative, and dangerous. When threatened, office wasps emit a chemical that alerts other wasps in the vicinity to become more aggressive and join the attack. Unlike bees, wasps can sting multiple times, and the repeated stings can cause anaphylactic shock that can lead to death.

Hornets are the largest of all wasp species and can prey on bees. It takes only a few large hornets to wipe out an entire beehive. Hornets even operate scout missions to seek out beehives.

This behavior and animosity is quite counterproductive to successful organizational output and performance in this sense. They do, however, serve an ecological purpose in that they keep insect pest populations at bay and are used more in the role of a policeman in organisations unlike their creative successful cousins, contributing further to the wasp's hostility.

### High Profile: Executioner Wasp (Polistes carnifex)

This small South America species of wasp has the most painful sting of all wasp species. The sting, which has been described as more severe than that of the bullet ant and killer bee, can render the victim debilitated for days at a time. The sting causes intense swelling and can be fatal if not treated properly.

Dealing with a Wasp

Interacting with a corporate wasp brings you in contact with their aggressive tendencies and makes you feel quite uncomfortable. They will often fly off the handle without warning, and this display can attract the wrath of other wasps nearby, so it is very important not to let this creature get upset in your presence. All tense situations should be immediately defused, and interactions should follow rigid preplanned guidelines. In another attempt to control a wasp's behavior, agendas should be sent in advance of any meeting so as not to catch the wasp by surprise. When you sense this natural aggression enter the discussion, try diverting the attention away to someone more mundane.

Trapping a Wasp

Corporate wasps, who are eternally living in the shadow of their corporate bee cousins, will always be attached to low-hanging fruit. This discovery and retrieval of low-hanging fruit (obtained without the same level of effort or ability exerted as bees) will be used as an attempt to gain the respect and admiration of their corporate colleagues. Wasps desperately strive to be held in the same regard as bees, but this is merely a dream because wasps cannot contribute successfully to any commercial venture and are never held in high regard by others, so their attempts are normally in vain.

In the wild, low-hanging fruit can be baited on top of jam jars, which will instinctively attract the wasp. Wasps will feed on this fruit and fall into the soapy solution in the jar below, rendering their wings immobile, resulting in their eventual drowning. This method can also be utilized in the corporate world, where clever baits are strategically placed for the wasp to "find," resulting in its eventual downfall owing to its lack of ability.

## Mosquitos and Flies (Diptera)

Flies are viewed as pests in the workplace; they are unproductive creatures that do not provide any positive output for the organization; they merely move from place to place causing contamination and disease and are always a drain on economic resources.

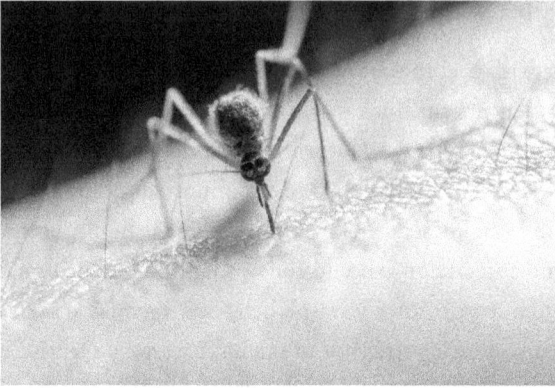

Mosquitos, however, are the deadliest creatures in the world; they cause more than one million human deaths every year worldwide. They spend their time moving from different contaminated surfaces and are carriers for multiple deadly diseases such as malaria and dengue fever.

Owing to their light and small stature, they land on the skin and draw blood, assisted by anticoagulant chemicals in their saliva, which keeps the wound from clotting. This process allows disease to enter the bloodstreams of the victim and, unfortunately, mosquitos are normally unassuming to most human beings.

Similar to conditions in the wild, corporate mosquitos are not tolerated and are sought out for eradication. They have a short life span, surviving usually only around eight weeks, and enter and leave organizations quite quickly, bringing with them their own level of toxins that cause imbalance to all organizations. Corporate Mosquitos never pass their probationary periods, but the damage they cause in such a short time has long-lasting effects for a corporation's performance.

Mosquitos are attracted by carbon dioxide and sweat and are therefore drawn to high-performing workers in an attempt to put them off course and cause major trouble.

Dealing with a Mosquito

Once a mosquito has been positively identified, you should never, under any circumstances, engage with this creature. You must cease all interactions and back away while alerting all in the immediate environment.

All identifications and sightings must then be immediately reported to the relevant senior management, and efforts must be made to remove them from the organization.

Trapping a Mosquito

In order to effectively remove mosquitos from an organization you must first effectively seek to remove their breeding grounds, which are normally damp stagnant environments. All toxicity in an area must be stamped out to ensure that they cannot return. Caution must be exercised not to smother the area in chemical repellents or insecticides because this will also eradicate other species of insect that are critical to the corporate environment's upkeep. An effective way to remove mosquitos actively is to extract them via air suction.

An effective device used in the wild is a common box fan, which normally force air into an environment, but the reverse side of these instruments actually suck up the air in a vacuumlike process in order to push it out again. A screen is then set over the fan's motor, which, essentially, catches and suspends these insects against the grill. This device can catch hundreds of mosquitos in a short time. The corporate equivalent of this is a companywide campaign to purge the organization of all pest behavior.

High Profile: (*Anopheles albimanus*)

These tiny unamusing insects, reaching lengths no larger than mere millimeters, are regarded as the most dangerous insect on earth. They are primary vectors for malaria and have contributed to more than 300 million transmissions each year worldwide and have led to 500,000 deaths each year.

They cause billions of dollars each year in worldwide treatment in associated medical costs.

## Butterflies and Moths (Including Caterpillars) (Lepidoptera)

Lepidoptera are a unique species within the corporate environment because they undergo a complete metamorphosis in such a short time. They

start life as caterpillars, causing havoc and sucking up all the resources and knowledge before completely changing into creatures capable of flight and moving to a different environment. Similarly, in the corporate world they start off in lower ranked positions and are fast-tracked to leadership positions.

Corporate Lepidoptera fall into two categories: they are either naturally extremely skilled and intelligent workers, capable of absorbing large amounts of information and then using it to rise up the corporate ranks or "selected" workers who are put on accelerated management courses or work experience by senior management in an attempt to mold them into specific senior roles.

As caterpillars they are inexperienced, their sole purpose being to eat and obtain nutrients. They are unable to see detailed images and can only differentiate between light and dark images. They stay in caterpillar form for normally four weeks before entering the chrysalis (butterfly) or cocoon (moth) stages. Corporate butterflies are charismatic and very important to organizations for their role in pollination, because they help other species to grow and prosper. They are important entities that hold organizations together.

Corporate moths, however, have a very different work life. They are not as favored as their butterfly cousins because they are not as unique (they outnumber butterflies ten to one, making them a sought-after food source for other species, particularly bats).

High Profile: *Assassin Caterpillar (Lonomia obliqua) Becomes the Giant Silkworm Moth*

This tiny caterpillar is the most venomous caterpillar on earth. Native to Brazil, it resides mainly on trees, blending in with its surroundings. Once touched, it transfers venom via multiple pinlike bristles that stick to the victim's skin. Once these bristles attach, they transfer toxins to the bloodstream containing anticlotting agents. This results in what looks like standard bruises to the victim, and their potential for danger is often overlooked. However, after 24 hours the toxins use up all the white blood cells and kill the victim (when it will be too late to administer the antivenom)

## Dealing with a Caterpillar and Moth

Dealing with a corporate caterpillar is usually a thankless and unrewarding task because it will seek only to benefit itself in any situation. They are information hoovers and will only seek to use this knowledge to advance themselves over a short time. It is ill-advised to withhold information from the caterpillar because it will use every resource to extract it from you.

It is best to just give them what they are looking for because they are present only for a very short time, and to deny them information only prolongs their presence, because deficient caterpillars do not enter the chrysalis phase required in order to become butterflies.

Dealing with a moth is similar to dealing with a caterpillar. Because moths have evolved and been propelled to senior positions of responsibility over a short time, they are essentially "Jack of all trades but masters of none." They can be easily distracted and will become confused and overly fixated in situations that require even the simplest of logic or problem-solving capabilities.

## Trapping a Caterpillar and Moth

As stated earlier, it is ill-advised to withhold information from a caterpillar because it will make your life miserable in its attempts to obtain it, this information being necessary to ensure its transformation. This is, however, how you actually expose it: You simply deny them the required information and weather the storm. If you can put up with its frantic attempts to source it, the caterpillar will eventually wither and die, not having achieved the chrysalis phase. This method will require extreme patience on your part, however, and is recommended only for the most resilient of corporate animals.

Trapping a moth can also be a tedious task. As mentioned earlier, they can become fixated on simple issues because, owing to their rapid advancement, they lack the correct expertise and problem-solving abilities required for their role.

Winged insects in the wild always use celestial light sources such as the sun or moon to guide their path, similarly to a textbook or manual that professionals will use to guide them on their journey. Moths (like their corporate counterparts), owing to their lack of expertise, cannot tell the difference between a natural and an artificial light source. So in times of change or unfamiliar situations they navigate toward artificial light sources and, unable to get their bearings at such a close distance, they fixate on the unnatural source and repeatedly circle and bump into the bulb. This is when they can be exposed and caught.

### Snails and Slugs (Gastropods)

Dealing with a corporate gastropod is an unusual affair. They are slow, slimy, and extremely frustrating to be around. These unusual creatures dislike sunlight and normally hide in the shade. Their slime is actually an adhesive allowing them to climb and stick to various surfaces, but it is also used for movement and to protect themselves when they move across dangerous surfaces.

Office gastropods use their slimy demeanors to protect themselves in virtually all encounters with other office species.

Snails are the most resilient of the species, having hard shells to hide in; when the going gets tough, however, slugs have to be more innovative to avoid predators.

Gastropods can also carry diseases, and it is very testing to be in their company for long periods, and you always leave an encounter feeling disgusted by the level of sliminess on display. This slime acts as a deterrent to office opponents, who do not wish to engage them unnecessarily, and allows the office gastropod to, essentially, have free rein and autonomy in projects because no one wants to be tainted by their slime.

## High Profile: Geographic Cone Snail (*Conus geographus*)

Found in the tropical reefs of Madagascar and Mauritius, these lightweight and often hidden small creatures are the most venomous snail species in the world. There is no known antivenom to this poisonous bite, which has resulted in multiple recorded human deaths over the last few decades.

## Dealing with a Snail

Long-term interaction with a corporate snail can have a detrimental effect on a person's image and reputation. Snails are seen as contributors to organizational failure and have normally dropped the ball some time ago on a critical project or initiative, and this fact is always remembered by all in the organisation.

Despite this fact, however, they are quite resilient and have managed to evade being fired, because insufficient evidence was available to lead to a prosecution or conviction. They have therefore been moved to a safe environment within many organizations where they can cause minimal damage. Interaction should be kept to a minimum, with written records kept of every encounter, because allowing a snail to become too involved in a project will almost certainly lead to its failure, and you will be held fully responsible.

Trapping a Snail

The sliminess of a snake can actually be used against it in many trapping or eradication scenarios. Salt is a key enemy of all snails because it, essentially, dries their skin out, resulting in their demise. Salt barriers are therefore quite effective to keep snails out of your business.

The corporate equivalent of salt barriers, in this example, are merely deterrents that will be off-putting to the snail and would consist of mirroring scenarios or replicating a similar environment where they have failed before, reminding them of the consequences of engaging you.

Corporate snails are always looking to redeem themselves of their past indiscretions and failures but will be averse to any painful reminder of failure in any newly presented scenario.

# Fish

Office fish are unique creatures insofar as they are limited to one environment, so if you encounter one, it will mean that you have strayed into their territory. This "limitation" can actually be a mastery because being adapted to one way of life is vital to organizational upkeep. Fish are a constant in any organization and are relied on as critical workers providing critical services. Because they do not sleep in ways that we traditionally associate with sleeping (fish's eyes are always open), they are no stranger to being on 24-hour call, and you will therefore usually find fish working in engineering, IT or finance departments. Fish "speak" to one another in their underwater environments through the use of sophisticated technical acoustic communication that only they can understand. Their decisions are widely accepted and valued, and fish are held in high regard as subject matter experts whom you defy at your own peril.

Fish are extremely knowledgeable and technical and thrive in organizations where methodical thinking is necessary for success. They do not fear change, but embrace it as a new challenge.

Fish have a deep sense of pride in their work, keep abreast of new legalization or innovations, and are usually financially secure.

However, they can be extremely dangerous and possess their own unique methods of attack, some proving fatal to anyone in their path. Some fish, as masters of their domain, are truly terrifying and are best avoided where possible.

Office fish can be categorized into two distinct groups:

1. **Cartilaginous Fish** (*Chondrichthyes*)
2. **Bony Fish** (*Osteichthyes*)

### Cartilaginous Fish: Sharks and Rays (Chondrichthyes)

This group of fish are arguably the deadliest of all fish. They lack a swim bladder for buoyancy and so must swim continuously to keep afloat and to force oxygen through their gills to breathe. If they stop swimming they die. Similarly to their office counterparts, they never rest and go to the bitter end to complete any task.

### Sharks (Selachimorpha)

Office sharks are apex predators of their aquatic environments and are designed to hunt.

They have a keen sense of hearing and are sensitive to vibrations given off by other fish in trouble. They can detect electrical signals emitted by vital organs of their prey and use these frequencies to home in on their victims. Office sharks are no different, being aggressive and quick to attack when they sense any weaknesses. They are meticulous in their actions and are consummate perfectionists, so if you make a mistake a shark will not let you forget it. They can sense fear and are attracted to situations where people are struggling. They have zero tolerance for learning on the job, and you must be able to hit the ground running when working with a shark. Like all cartilaginous fish, they must keep swimming in order to breathe and stay afloat, so they are relentless in their actions, never letting up or taking breaks. They travel vast distances and never sleep and so are revered by senior management for their commitment and dedication. Their one downfall, however, is that they are adapted to only certain environments and can survive only in familiar territory. Sharks are normally found in heads of department roles and normally thrive in high-pressure environments that are critical to overall organizational performance.

## High Profile: Bull Shark (*Carcharhinus leucas*)

Reaching lengths of up to 8 ft, this species of shark has the strongest bite of all shark species. Found regularly in the Amazon River, they are unique in that they can move between salt water and fresh water with ease and are responsible for most attacks on humans.

## Dealing with a Shark

Interactions with a shark usually benefit only one party, that party being the shark. In order to engage a shark, you must go to its territory, so you are automatically at a disadvantage. These apex predators do not discriminate, so they will not hesitate to attack you on sight. Interactions are normally quite rapid, with sharks making their intention known from the outset. They will sense fear and weakness in any encounter and will home in on these vulnerabilities immediately. Therefore, it is advisable to ensure that you have all perceived bases covered before you approach a shark. Do not leave any loose ends, and always ensure that you have carried out all the activities necessary to complete your part of the interaction. Never put an activity on the long finger when dealing with a shark because this will only incense them. The main rule when engaging a shark is to get in and get out as quickly as possible, not stick around, deal in facts only, and always "dot your i's and cross your t's" before you arrive at their department.

Trapping a Shark

Trapping a shark is not for the fainthearted. It can be performed only by the most fearless individuals and usually requires a team. This process should not be tried without the proper precautions. Sharks are lured in the wild by a process known as "chumming," in which blood and other fish guts are dumped into the water, attracting the sharks in the vicinity. Hence, a situation must be orchestrated whereby the corporate shark perceives a struggle or someone in distress.

As soon as they arrive on the scene, they need be secured with nets and immediately turned upside down. Turning a shark upside down renders the shark in a trancelike state known as "tonic immobility," and this is when the shark can be easily managed and exposed. Turning a corporate shark upside down is essentially making them move in motions that they are not used to. This can be done only by taking them out of their comfort zone and into scenarios where they are in unnatural territory.

### Rays (Batoidea)

This species of fish is also extremely deadly. They possess long barbed tails containing powerful toxins that are used to ward off attackers and to subdue their prey.

Rays use electrosensors to locate prey, similar to those of sharks, and are attracted to movement and vibrations given off by their prey. Like sharks, they are mostly solitary and can travel vast distances but normally hide at the bottom of rivers.

Office rays are no different, they stay out of view and attack when you least expect it. Office rays are quite unassuming and, because of their flat appearance and low profile close to the bottom of rivers, are often over-looked as being dangerous. They are usually stepped on by others in the office, and this is where they are at their most dangerous.

## High Profile: Blue spotted Ribbon tail Ray (*Taeniura lymma*)

This relatively small fish found in the reefs of Madagascar has a shy de-meanor but a deadly sting. It has two extremely venomous spines near the middle of the tail that, when used, can inflict serious pain on humans.

## Dealing with a Ray

Unfortunately, most people don't realize that they are interacting with a ray until it is too late. They are often overlooked because of their unas-suming and shy demeanor, but this is what makes them so deadly. It is advisable to shuffle your feet when entering bodies of water to alert them to your presence. Analogously, corporate rays should be approached in the same manner, ostentatiously alerting them to your arrival to ensure that they are not accidentally stepped on, in order to avoid a nasty sting in the process.

## Trapping a Ray

Sting rays reside almost exclusively in shallow waters, so despite it being hard to see sometimes because of their camouflage techniques, their fa-vorite dwelling places are often always a known fact. Rays do not like to enter deep water because they are hunted by much larger and fiercer fish, so they spend their time in shallower waters near riverbanks where there are fewer predators.

Being easy to locate and access therefore makes them easy to capture with spears or nets.

Corporate rays, like their wild counterparts, are not difficult to catch because their location is always known. You must be cautious, however, in your choice of capture method, because a net is the most useful in avoiding any unwanted stings.

### Bony Fish (Osteichthyes)

This group of fish differ from their cartilaginous cousins by the simple fact that they have a skeleton made of bone and possess swim bladders and so do not have to swim in order to breathe and stay afloat. Smaller fish in this group tend to congregate in groups for protection.

### Piranha (Serrasalmidae)

The name *piranha* literally translates as "tooth fish" in the native Tupi language. These fearsome predators have razor-sharp teeth, which they use to attack the tails and eyes of their victims, rendering them immobile and unable to get away before they are completely consumed.

Office piranhas are no different than their wild counterparts insofar as they are small and like to stay in groups for protection because they are not apex predators but have many predators.

Piranhas normally operate hierarchy systems, with younger more mobile fish staying on the outside of the group, being the first line of defense, and the older, less mobile fish staying in the center of the group, usually for protection and also for directing the attacks or movements of the school.

Piranhas are attracted by noise, blood, and movement within their environments. Being a highly aggressive species, they normally turn on themselves if there is insufficient prey available, so there will always be disputes among office piranha teams unless they are in a constant state of war with other species. They are bound by animosity, and their bonds, being weak, are easily broken. Office groups of piranhas have extremely stressful and unhealthy working environments because they are, essentially, a group of people with a chip on their shoulders looking to seek vengeance on anyone that they can find.

### High Profile: Red-bellied Piranhas (*Pygocentrus nattereri*)

Native to Brazil, these small fish of Hollywood fame have stronger jaws and sharper teeth than any other species of piranha. Traveling in groups, they use these razor-sharp teeth to collectively shred their prey within a matter of seconds.

### Dealing with a Piranha

All interactions with a piranha normally results in the involvement of other piranha because they are not solitary creatures, so you should never interact with piranha on your own.

There is safety in numbers, so make sure, when interacting with corporate piranha, that you have a team with you. This team will not stop the aggressive tendencies that will ultimately follow, but it may make the piranha less likely to attack a larger entity. It is also important to understand a piranha's activities and habits, because they will hunt only in daylight hours, and so it may be more effective to catch a piranha outside the 9 through 5 window, when their aggression is somewhat reduced. Piranhas are also drawn to blood, so it is important not to approach them if you are injured or display any sign of vulnerabilities whatsoever. They are also attracted to a fuss or energetic behavior, so you must always appear calm and collected in their presence to avoid any attack.

### Trapping a Piranha

When looking to capture a piranha, a normal fishing line is simply not strong enough, so a reinforced steel leader is always advisable. The only bait that is effective in luring these creatures is raw flesh, mirroring the corporate world, where corporate piranhas can also be lured to a specific location by baiting these areas with the appropriate bait; once corralled into an area their exits can be blocked, and they can be caught much more easily.

## Mammals

Office Mammals can be categorized into eight distinct groups:

1. **Rodents** (*Rodentia*)
2. **Bats** (*Chiroptera*)
3. **Shrews and Hedgehogs** (*Eulipotyphla*)
4. **Sloths and Anteaters** (*Pilosa*)
5. **Apes and Monkeys** (*Primates*)
6. **Hoofed Animals** (*Ungulates*)
7. **Elephants** (*Elephantidae*)
8. **Meat-eating predators** (*Carnivora*)

### Rodents: Mice, Rats, Beavers (Rodentia)

Office rodents are typified by their incisor teeth, which are continually growing. Stemming from the Latin word, *rodere*, meaning "to gnaw," rodents must constantly bite and chew objects in order to keep their teeth short and manageable. They are extremely social animals with a high level of intelligence but are extremely difficult to work with in an office setting.

Rats are naturally sneaky; they are able to recognize close relatives by smell and single them out for preferential treatment regarding food, so an office rat will always try and recruit family or friends into key positions.

Rats also harbor disease, and being around one for too long will make you both physically and mentally sick. When rats are introduced to a new environment, they quickly disperse or eradicate all native fauna because of the strain that they put on their resources. This explains why staff turnover is so high in departments led by corporate rats.

Studies have also shown that rats in the wild are vulnerable to peer pressure and so often engage in activities or eating food that they normally do not like in order to "show face" within their unit or sociable group. This explains why office rats seem to go along with whatever scheming plan that one member of their group has orchestrated.

Office mice, however, are less intimidating, being smaller in stature and less scheming. They look for heat and food and generally do not want to draw any attention to themselves. Mice will normally keep to the perimeter of a room in order to avoid detection and do not like being in the spotlight.

Office beavers, however, are an entirely different rodent than their rat and mouse cousins. These animals have a powerful visual impact on the office environment through the construction of their dams. These dams not only direct river flows but can also create new plant life and wetlands in the vicinity of the structure. These dams, however, are not always welcome and can be detrimental to many office ecosystems. It must be noted, however, that dam construction is an entirely selfish act and is undertaken only to assist beavers with their own living conditions, because they require a body of still water to build their homes.

High Profile: Black Rats: (*Rattus rattus*—Invasive species)

The common Black rat, nothing more, nothing less—how is this species worthy of a profile spot in a list normally typified by the most deadly and fearsome predators on earth? The answer: They are infamous pests that were indirectly responsible for over 200 million deaths linked to the bubonic plague in medieval times. Although not responsible for transmitting the disease to humans themselves, they carried the fleas that did the damage. Modern day rats also carry disease, and their urine can cause Weil's disease, which can cause death or long-term effects.

## Dealing with a Rat

Ideally, no one likes to deal with a rat, but, unfortunately, because rats are found in many corporations worldwide, these interactions are unavoidable. Corporate rats are calculating, self-serving, and significantly damaging to morale in a workplace. A rat will always try to cause controversy and will normally complain to your line manager about something that you did or did not do.

These traits make people wary of rats and determined to avoid them at all costs. When dealing with a rat, however, you must be aware of their specific character and understand their history, and you must seek to establish who their allies and enemies are within the organization.

One effective adaptation of survival when dealing with a rat is to fool it into thinking that you are on their side but always remain at a far enough distance to not to be sucked into their world.

You need to use all your political ingenuity when dealing with corporate rats because they can be detrimental to your career and have a negative bearing on your mental health and well-being.

## Trapping a Rat

When trapping a rat, you must be aware of and respect its level of intelligence. Rats will normally not approach new items in their environment such as traps because they will have a natural fear of the unknown. You must lure the rat into a false sense of security in order to effectively catch it.

Traps must be baited but not set so that the rat can easily access the food and be accustomed to its presence; when the rat has become overly familiar with the trap, that is the time to set it and catch the rat.

This can also be applied to corporate rats, as mentioned earlier; you can lure them into a false sense of security by pretending to be on their side, and once they do not perceive you as a threat they will feel comfortable in your presence, where they will then expose their true character. At this stage you record every wrongdoing and gather evidence on their unscrupulous activities. You can choose to either turn them in or use this evidence as ammunition to ensure the rat stays out of your way.

## *Bats* (Chiroptera*)*

Bats are extremely important to office environments because they can eat over one thousand mosquitos in the space of just a few short hours. The digestive system of a bat is also finely tuned to enrich various types of seeds, and many seeds will not grow fully unless they have passed through a bat's digestive system first. Being blind does not hinder their performance, because using highly sophisticated echo sound, they are even able to distinguish between poisonous and nonpoisonous animals just by listening to their calls. Office bats, like their wild counterparts, are no different; they are able to gauge threats and are so finely tuned to the office environment that they can differentiate between individual employees just by listening to their breathing. Bats, however, can be extremely dangerous because they carry diseases. This association with sickness often precedes them, so they are rarely welcomed into senior leadership positions. They are the most underutilized employees in any organization, never reaching their full potential and so are indirectly forced to retreat into the darkness, where they contemplate how they can help improve their image.

High Profile: Hairy-Legged Vampire Bats (*Diphylla ecaudata*)

This winged assassin is the stuff of horror movies, with its menacing demeanor and sharp fangs, but, more importantly, it feasts solely on blood, including human blood. They also carry disease, so a bite can normally lead to rabies.

### Dealing with a Bat

When dealing with a bat it is important to realize that you are dealing with a highly intelligent species, so do not underestimate them on the basis of their reputations as outcasts.

Despite this intelligence and as a consequence of the years of social outcasting, bats have developed a low sense of confidence and self-esteem. They will be overly cautious and sensitive in many situations, but do not conflate this behavior with any physical or mental vulnerabilities, because a corporate bat can tie you in knots and cause serious damage when it attacks you, so caution should always be exercised when interacting with this species.

### Trapping a Bat

As stated earlier, bats are quite sensitive and lack self-confidence, so they are always at a disadvantage when in the spotlight. This is similar to bats in the wild in that they will always fear and try to avoid unnatural light sources. Being nocturnal, they prefer to hide in the shadows, so if you ever wish to expose a corporate bat or render it immobile you must ensure that it is the focus of everyone's attention. This could mean simply giving the bat public praise for any achievement that it has brought to the organization. This will make the bat self conscious and be in a state of disorientation for some time where its guard is considerably lowered.

### *Shrews and Hedgehogs* (Eulipotyphla)

Shrews are wired, wired to the point that their heart beats 1,000 times a minute and they make over ten body movements per second. They are always in a frenzy. The reason for this frantic behavior is that if they do not eat within two hours they will die. Office shrews are no different; they frantically traverse the office in a fluster, reminding stakeholders of their obligations to an initiative to ensure a project's deadline is met. If a milestone passes without completion, a shrew will suffer great anxiety. They can cause nightmares for any project team with their tendency to hound you until you give them the information that they need or complete a task that is critical to their initiative, but they can also be a positive attribute if they are on your side.

Shrews, however, can also be extremely deadly. They possess toxins, sometimes enough to kill hundreds of mice. They also have toxins in their saliva that render its prey immobile.

Corporate hedgehogs are less frantic. Like their shrew cousins, they have extremely poor eyesight but differ in that they are not toxic. They do, however, possess an armory of 5,000 quills that they use for defense when attacked by predators. They are unique insofar as they are immune to most snake venom.

## High Profile: Thor's Hero Shrew (*Scutisorex thori*)

This tiny mammal, native to the Congo rain forest, is only a foot long but is the only mammal known to have interlocked vertebrae, allowing it to hold the record for having the strongest back of all mammals in the world relative to its size (up to four times stronger than humans). It uses this strength to lift rocks and logs to get to its prey. It is named after the mystical superhero Thor.

## Dealing with a Shrew

Corporate Shrews are meticulously frantic creatures, always on the hunt for information.

As stated earlier, shrews possess potent toxins that can render their prey immobile; the prey is then taken back to the nest, ensuring that the shrew has a meal for later in the evening...so it's best to give them the information that they need and let them be on their way.

Trapping a Shrew

Trapping a shrew is an unnecessary task because if you simply give them what they want they will simply move on, but for whatever reason you wish to trap a shrew the most effective way is as follows:

As previously explained, a shrew must eat every few hours or it will die. The corporate equivalent of this when a shrew is frantically pursuing information that is not provided on time will have an anxiety attack. So this is effectively how to trap them. You simply withhold the relevant information that they deem critical to their project. Let me clarify, however, that the critical information that the shrew requires might actually not be critical to the project because it may merely be a figment of the corporate shrew's obsessive-compulsive disorder (OCD), so always display caution when withholding any information that is deemed project critical. Once a shrew has been disappointed by you, they will not usually reengage you.

### Sloths and Anteaters (Pilosa)

*Pilosa* are a species of animal that share similar characteristics but are sometimes a world apart from each other.

### Anteaters

These ground-dwelling creatures have evolved over time to be effective at one type of hunting technique, which is to eat ants (and termites) inside their mounds, which their long snout adaptation makes possible.

Corporate anteaters are also only adept at one main skill set, which, however, they perform much better than anyone else in the organization. They are subject matter experts and will be called upon to deal with the most complex issues when something goes wrong. They are also extremely adept in finding solutions to problems (within their skill set) where none were thought possible and are held in high regard as natural problem solvers by all within the corporate world, viewing them as successful and influential members of any team.

### Sloths

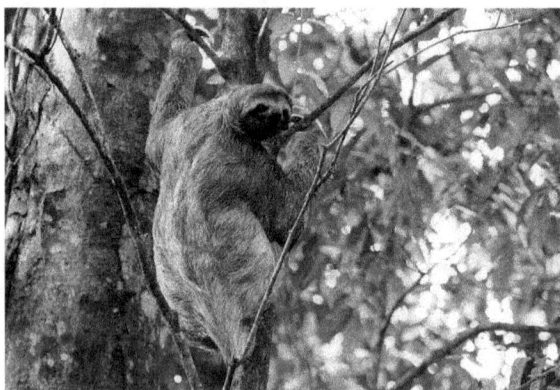

Corporate Sloths are the poor cousins of anteaters, because despite having a specialty in gripping and climbing, they choose not to use their skills for advancement but to sit stationary, with algae even growing on their fur in the wild. Corporate sloths are the members of the team who refuse to innovate or show initiative and are always the slowest to respond to change, not out of inability, but just as a result of their personalities. They lack motivation and drive and are in the job only because they have failed at their true goal in life due to laziness. They are, essentially, the failed rock stars of the corporate world because they possess talent but do not show it in the corporate environment.

Sloths in the wild can move twice as fast when swimming but rarely do this, so we can see that corporate sloths are perhaps just in the wrong environment.

Regardless of the reason for their lack of motivation, they are extremely hard to deal with and will show an indifference or disdain to your requests or enthusiasm in getting tasks completed.

## Dealing with a Pilosa

**Anteater**: Dealing with an anteater is actually a pleasure, because they are an inspiration to watch and will always provide pragmatic solutions to your problems. You must, however, always seek to match their level of commitment, or they will become frustrated and will often wrongly mistake your inability to keep up with them for a lack of motivation and may de-prioritize your request for assistance.

**Sloth:** When dealing with a sloth, especially if you need information from them, you must realize that it will take quite some time because they sleep up to 18 hours per day and are only active for very short periods. Sloths, owing to their disdain for anything positive, will normally work to rule and become jobsworths. You must remember to plan this bottleneck well in advance of any programme creation and always to be patient in their presence because any attempts to speed up the process with aggression will only lead to longer delays. You must seek to find common interests with the sloth on a personal level away from the corporate world, usually music or movies, which you may have in common. This will show the sloth that it can relate to someone and lead to higher than usual levels of satisfaction to aid in your quest for obtaining information or input from them.

## Trapping a Pilosa

### Anteater

When seeking to trap or expose an anteater, you must be aware that the consequences can be fatal. An anteater, as we have discussed, is a subject matter expert in its field, so any attempts to outsmart them in this regard will be futile. The only really effective way to trap an anteater is to seek to take it out of its comfort zone. Examples of these opportunities usually present themselves in cross-function teams, where duties and responsibilities are sometimes not as demarcated as they are within to 'one on one' interactions.

The anteater must be given incremental responsibilities so subtle as not to be detected at first and add more at a quicker rate once it is comfortable. This will disorientate the anteater and expose a weakness, which is that they are hardwired to dealing with only one large issue in isolation and not multiple small issues simultaneously.

## Sloths

The personality of a corporate sloth is, essentially its armor; sloths do not possess the same emotional attachment or pride in their work that other animals possess, so trapping them can be quite difficult. They are safe in their environment high up in the trees. Sloths, however, have another weakness beyond their slow movement, which is the need to climb down from trees to relieve themselves. This is when the most attacks on sloths occur because they are outwitted and outmaneuvered by predators when they leave the sanctity of their tree. You must therefore seek to remove a sloth from the safety of their environment. This is usually when they are not protected by policy and forced to think on their feet. The only way to do this, unfortunately, is to give them more responsibility and autonomy, making them accountable for their own decisions. They will not like this and display vulnerability, allowing them to be exposed.

## High Profile: Giant Anteater (*Myrmecophaga tridactyla*)

The largest in the anteater family, native to South America, this species can grow up to 7 feet in length and weigh up to 50 kg; it has a distinctive long snout and powerful sharp jaws.

## High Profile: Brown-Throated Sloth (*Bradypus variegatus*)

This tree-dwelling creature can grow up to 80 cm and weigh up to 6 kg. It has powerful sharp claws, allowing it to hang effectively.

*Hoofed Animals* (ungulates)

Hoofed animals are in demand in the jungle environment but for all the wrong reasons. These graceful herbivores are always the meal for larger fiercer predators. Their only defense is to stay out of view or run. Having eyes on the side of their heads to improve lookout capabilities, pointed ears, and also legs adapted for forward and backward motion, these animals are designed to be anonymous and escape tight situations. The hooves of these animals also continually grow, so movement is required to keep them maintained and ultimately necessary to ensure the animals' survival.

Corporate Deer are naturally nervous and cautious in every aspect of their work life. They fear being targeted and will often freeze in dense undergrowth when larger predators are in the vicinity. Hoofed animals usually possess horns and antlers, which they use for defense and interspecies fighting, but these weapons are no match for their predators. Hoofed animals usually travel in pairs for company. This is similar to corporate hoofed animals because having a companion to go with for a smoke or a coffee lowers their anxiety levels. Corporate hoofed animals have no interest in getting top positions in the boardroom; they merely wish to be left alone to do their work and focus more on their lives outside the company.

High Profile: Okapi (*Okapia johnstoni*)

Native only to the Congo rain forest, the okapi are so well adapted to survival that when they are born they do not defecate for one month so as not to attract predators. For the same reason, baby okapis communicate with their mothers via infrasound, which is beyond the normal hearing range of their predators.

## Dealing with a Hoofed Animal

Hoofed animals are a nervous bunch, constantly on the lookout for predators and ready to flee at every given turn, so interacting with them can be highly problematic. They normally lack the self-confidence required to successfully carry out tasks and will normally need to be assisted along the way. At the slightest indication of pressure, a hoofed animal will normally be rendered ineffective on project-based activities, so care must be taken when giving them responsibilities. Hoofed animals in all departments display identical traits and, being overly cautious, will not stick their heads above the parapets to make decisions. They are ruled by fear and will always pass the buck when any important decisions need to be made. The only effective solution that there is to this kind of behavior is to engage them well ahead of time so that they can decide in advance whom they wish to pass the buck to, effectively ensuring that your project is not affected.

## Trapping a Hoofed Animal

Trapping hoofed animals has normally been a straightforward process because of the visible presence of tracks, but, sadly, this is not the case in the jungle, where leaf litter and dense undergrowth imprint tracks poorly or even not at all. Hoofed animals in the jungle are also adapted to blend into their environments, making them even harder to locate and trap.

The only way to successfully trap a hoofed animal is to successfully lure it from its hiding place. In order to do this, you must blend into the environment as much as possible and make yourself as unassuming as you can. You must avoid potent smells and unnecessary sounds, and once camouflaged you stand a better chance of seeing the animal emerge from hiding. Corporate hoofed animals are exactly the same in that if you are deemed a threat, they will flee, so the trick is to make yourself as inconspicuous as possible, gain their trust, and then strike.

## *Elephants* (Elephantidae)

Elephants, although not a million miles away from ungulates, are actually referred to as Paenungulates ("almost ungulates") because they have large flat feet rather than traditional hooves.

They still, however, merit a category all by themselves

Elephants are indisputably astounding creatures, being symbols of strength, endurance, and intelligence. They are also extremely sentient beings, with a vast array of feelings and emotions, and simply being in their presence is truly awe inspiring and motivational.

The same is true for corporate elephants, who are held in such high esteem by their peers and seen so much as people that they aspire to be in their careers. Elephants in the rain forests, like their corporate counterparts, are pioneers in that they literally break down barriers and shape paths for other animals to travel on.

Elephants are extremely sociable animals and can communicate over large distances using subsonic sounds that travel through the earth.

Despite their large size, they are extremely graceful; their trunks are sensitive enough to pick up a single blade of grass but also strong enough to break branches from powerful trees. The corporate elephant is no different, having the skills, concentration, and intelligence of a talented surgeon yet possessing the muscle and resolve of an Olympic weightlifter. This versatility, along with the fact that they can see equally perfectly both during the day and at night, makes them adaptable to any work-related task and ultimately contributes to their herolike status within the workplace.

High Profile: African Forest Elephant (*Loxodonta cyclotis*)

Native only to the Congo rain forest, this species is the smallest of all elephant species, yet is still one of the largest mammals on earth.

This smaller size is an adaptation that allows them to move through the dense jungle more easily.

## Dealing with an Elephant

Dealing with an elephant can be an extremely intimidating prospect at first, but the more time you spend in its presence the more it will amaze you. Corporate elephants are highly intelligent and experienced creatures and possess high morals and standards.

They are impressive, and you will normally come away from an encounter somewhat enlightened or inspired.

## Trapping an Elephant

Trapping an elephant is not normally recommended in view of their sheer size and strength, but there may be cases in which you need to carry out this task.

Elephants in the wild are corralled into man-made traps, known as "Khedda traps," which are essentially traps made of bamboo or wood with 12-feet-high walls that are pulled in place by ropes. This process is usually coordinated by a team of people in order to be effective, so in order to trap an elephant you cannot work alone. Elephants need to be enticed, lured, or driven into position, and this is not for the fainthearted.

Making an elephant move into these traps is an operation usually led by a man atop a domesticated elephant, known as a "mahout." Once the elephant sees that it is being led by another elephant, it instinctively trusts its own species. The key here, then, with corporate elephants is to infiltrate their group and use a member as a lure.

## *Apes and Monkeys* (Primates)

Primates are made up of four distinct groups:

1. **Great apes: Gorillas, Chimpanzees, Bonobos and ... Humans**

2. **Lesser apes: Gibbons**
3. **Monkeys**
4. **Prosimians: Lemurs**

Primates are extremely sociable animals that live in groups with hierarchical structures and have advanced communication systems, and include some of the most intelligent animals on the planet.

## Great Apes

**Gorillas** are extremely powerful creatures and are really only annoyed by other gorillas. The alpha male is usually the strongest and most powerful of the group, whose presence is enough to stop any dispute breaking out within the group. Corporate gorillas are no different, their powerful and intimidating behavior encourages everyone else to fall in line.

High Profile: Eastern lowland gorilla (*Gorilla beringei graueri*)

Native only to the Congo rain forests, the eastern lowland gorilla are the largest primates on earth. Weighing up to 200 kg and standing over 6 feet, they are a force to be reckoned with.

Chimpanzees

Gorilla behavior differs to chimpanzees however, who despite also living in hierarchical structures, the alpha male chimpanzee is not always the strongest. He can become the alpha by being the most popular member of the group backed by his allies or by scheming his way to the top using underhanded political tactics—sounds familiar?

High Profile: The Central Chimpanzee/Tschego (*Pan troglodytes troglodytes*)

Indigenous to the rain forest of central Africa, these are the largest species of chimpanzees in the world.

Bonobos

Bonobos, by comparison with other great apes, are known for their diplomatic, graceful, and mainly peaceful coexistence. This is the corporate equivalent of the office intelligentsia groups with many new age and politically conscientious learned people.

High Profile: African Bonobo (*Pan paniscus*)

Found only in the Congo, this species of ape, although not the loudest, has the widest range of vocalizations of all primates in the world and communicates via a vast arrangement of vocalizations, emphasizing various kinds of information.

## Lesser Apes

Gibbons

Gibbons are known as lesser apes, primarily because they are smaller than their "greater ape" counterparts. Being smaller, however, has its benefits, gibbons being the fastest of all the apes (Greater and Lesser), and are known to swing through the trees at speeds of up to 40 mph.

Office Gibbons are no different; they use this speed to compensate for their lesser "ape strength" and will often boast of being able to complete tasks quicker and more efficiently than anyone else.

High Profile: Siamang (*Symphalangus syndactylus*)

This species of primate, native to the jungles of Sumatra, are the largest of the "Lesser Apes." They are also the only gibbon species to possess a "gular sac," which is inflated to give their calls more range and volume.

## Monkeys

Monkeys, by comparison with apes, are smaller and faster. They have prehensile tails and are normally louder than apes. Office monkeys know that

they are not as powerful or as influential as their ape counterparts, a fact, however, that they usually don't accept publicly, portraying themselves as just as worthy of the ape accolades. The male howler monkey has the record of the loudest call of any other known primate. Incidentally, scientists have now linked this behavior to smaller genitalia and lower sperm count of the individual monkey. Wait! So in order to overcompensate for small genitalia, the males of this species are overly loud and lairy to divert attention away from this embarrassing shortcoming? Sounds familiar?

High Profile: Guatemalan black howler Monkey (*Alouatta pigra*)

Native to the rain forests of Guatemala and Belize, the Guatemalan Black Howler is the largest of all howler monkey species, spending most of the day resting and eating and the remainder of the day screaming from the treetops as a show of strength.

### *Prosimians*

Lemurs

Lemurs are the odd one out in this setup, as despite having many characteristics common to other primates, specifically monkeys, they get a bad rap and are viewed by people in a very different way than other primates. The name "lemur" literally translates as "evil spirit of the dead," and they are feared by many locals in their native Madagascar as having supernatural capabilities.

Office lemurs are feared, in equal measure, as having unorthodox and unusual styles and are often pushed out of departments or organizations because of these unorthodox styles or for simply being different.

High Profile: Aye (*Daubentonia madagascariensis*)

This unusual creature, found only in Madagascar, is more suited to a horror movie with is menacing appearance and skeletonlike long fingers. It is the largest nocturnal primate in the world, but, contrary to its appearance, is an omnivore and actually quite peaceful. It lives a solitary lifestyle but is threatened by humans who seek it out for destruction owing to their fears and superstitious beliefs.

Dealing with a Primate

When dealing with corporate primates, whether large or small, it is always advisable to have a clear objective in mind. Do not rely on them to guide you on the success of a project because they will only seek to benefit from its fruits. Despite the presence of hierarchical systems, the politics at play in primate cultures is the highest of all species, and coups d'états are sporadically entertained. So it is important to have strong convictions and an escape plan when dealing with these creatures. Primate politics can be deadly even if you remain neutrally aware, so it is best not to even acknowledge (to any primate) that these political endeavours actually exist, because acknowledgment will result in your ultimately being forced to pick a side.

(See Chapter 5 for further details on how to deal with a primate)

## Trapping a Primate

Trapping a primate will always have political consequences, so you must remain hidden in your endeavors. In the wild, apes and monkeys are captured almost exclusively by blow darts and netting.

Please refer to Chapter 5 for further information on how to trap a primate.

### Meat-Eating Predator Cats (Carnivora feliformia)

Jungles have two apex predators that will never ever cross paths owing to their geographic position; the jaguar is native to South and Central America, while the tiger is native to Asia.

Both animals, however, are at the top of their food chains in their environments.

### Tigers (Panthera tigris)

### Sumatran Tigers (Panthera tigris sondaica)

Confined to the small island of Sumatra, these powerful creatures are under severe threat of extinction, with less than 400 individuals estimated to be left in the wild. Tigers are solitary ambush predators that meticulously stalk their prey and pounce with savage might. They can run up to 40 mph, and absolutely nothing is outside of their range of hunting capabilities. Corporate tigers are feared and revered in equal measure, but they are viewed as a dying breed in boardrooms across the world. They are rarely spotted in day- to-day operations and have a somewhat mythical persona and reputation. To see one in action is an unforgettable experience. They are viewed as living legends, are often founders of many successful organizations, and are promoted worldwide as symbols of ferocity and corporate drive. They hold chairperson or presidential roles within organizations but rarely CEO positions. They are fantastic from a PR perspective and portray a strong corporate image, but do not write these animals off as merely a relic of good times gone by, because they are still the most fearsome predator in their environment and will not let you forget it.

## Dealing with a Tiger

When dealing with a tiger you must understand that you are dealing with an icon. This person is not only powerful and respected almost universally, but has built the very organization that pays your salary, so respect must always be given. The contrast between its majestic grace and sheer wild strength is also mesmerizing and you will always be inspired when dealing with a corporate tiger.

## Trapping a Tiger

Trapping a corporate tiger is a quest that few would ever dream of undertaking. Similar to trapping corporate eagles, and owing to their iconic position, any attempts to take them down are considered a coup d'état and will always lead to a regime change.

You should always proceed with caution, but remember that I told you that this was a bad idea…

All felines, whether wild or domesticated, have a peculiar affinity for boxes. Yes, that's right, your standard run-of-the-mill cardboard box is revered by cats big and small all over the world. The reasons for this affinity are still debated by scientists today. One school of thought attributes the box to the security that the animal can achieve while hidden away from view and out of stressful situations, whereas others attribute this behavior to cats and their ambush predatory traits, so concealment by boxes is a natural fit.

Wild tigers in Sumatra are captured, therefore, by box traps in which live bait is placed in a large rectangular box, and when the tiger enters, the door closes shut behind it, trapping it inside. This is how corporate tigers are also captured, their innate biological behavior is used against them in order to trap them. Whether this means exploiting their power, charity, or ego, it can always be weaponized against them in some form.

### Jaguars (Panthera onca)

These animals are, essentially, the complete package, being apex predators in the Amazon that are virtually unbeatable. Despite being the third largest cats in the world (behind lions and tigers), they make up for it by possessing the strongest bite of any cat predator in the world and attack exclusively by crushing the skull of their prey rather than going for the neck like other big cats in their feliform group.

Owing to their stubborn, determined, and elusive personalities, they are the only cat that cannot be tamed, cannot be broken, and are virtually indestructible. You would never have seen a jaguar at a circus.

Jaguars are solitary creatures with excellent climbing skills and live in territories marked out by claw marks warning other animals not to enter their domain. Corporate jaguars are almost exclusively CEOs within many organizations. They command and receive respect at every juncture.

Dealing with a Jaguar

The success of a jaguar in the corporate world is mainly attributable to two key facts. The first is its obvious abilities, but the other, attributed to its success is its lack of ego (or as we have learned earlier in the chapter, it's ego is in perfect balance!).

Jaguars, despite being the wildest of all wild animals, are impossible to tame, are incredibly shy and reserved creatures, and behave in an unassuming manner, blending into the background and never appearing flashy. This is because they do not have to. The jaguar has achieved its position via results that require talent, power, and intelligence and does not need to overcompensate with theatrics and charades to appear powerful because it knows that it is already powerful, as does everyone else. Interacting with a jaguar can be quite confusing however for the uninitiated because they sometimes mistake its sense of humility for a weakness...and God help them...

Trapping a Jaguar

Possibly the most dangerous trap ever to be set in the corporate world. The difficulty, however, does not lie in the setting of the trap but in what you intend to do once you've trapped the jaguar.

A simple foot loop trap is the best way to capture jaguars in the wild because they cause relatively zero harm to the animal, merely rendering them immobile. Now what do you do, you ask? Good question, for in the wild the jaguar is then subdued with a blow dart to successfully allow the handlers to carry out medical or tracking tasks. In the corporate world, however, the jaguar is now trapped by the foot, looking at everyone trying to figure out who is responsible and has already worked it out.

You must have irrefutable evidence to attempt a move like this because it will, essentially, be like a coup d'état in overthrowing a government or a monarchy: You may incur the wrath of other invading organizations that view your company as a destabilized weaker entity.

Once you have identified and profiled your opponent, you will now need to look for patterns within their movement. These patterns will reveal their motivations and help understand their behavior.

When seeking to understand movement, we must turn our attention to the science behind our movements.

In the early 20th century a French mathematician, by the name of Paul Levy, studied the statistical probabilities of movement in an attempt to reveal patterns of motion behavior. This research was then applied to field biology in order to study the foraging techniques of animals and their ultimate effectiveness.

This study eventually culminated in the emergence of what is known as the "levy flight foraging hypothesis."

The results reveal that when animals hunt, they all seem to follow patterns of short random movements in a small geographical area, and when the resources have been either expended or not found they then move in a random path or trajectory characterized by one long linear unbroken movement. Once arrived at the new destination, they adopt the same search of a small geographical area until food is found, not found, or depleted and then move away again in a long linear unbroken trajectory. This pattern is repeated ad infinitum.

The following is an example of the levy flight foraging hypothesis:

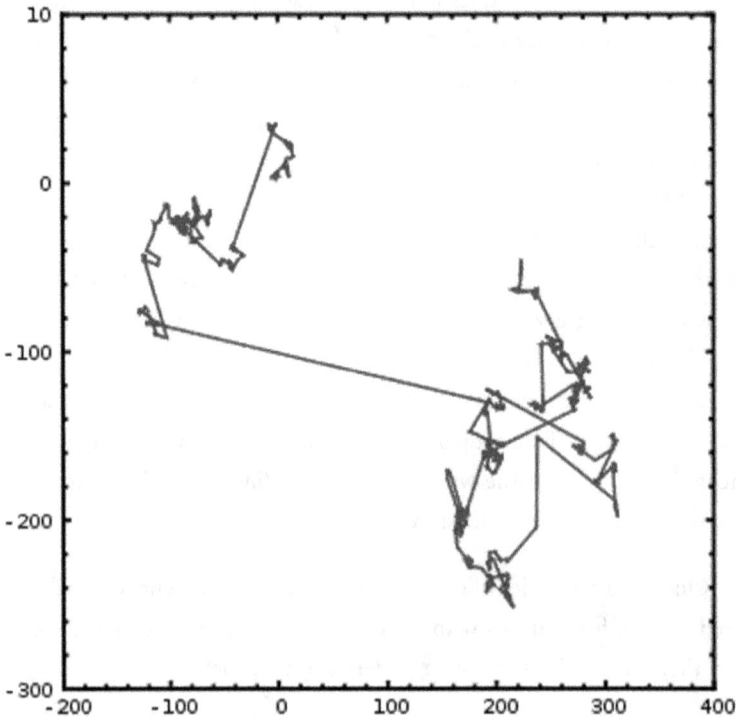

When seeking to understand human behavior in the corporate world, we can seek to apply the same logic.

An employee will pursue a prize, a promotion, for example, and focus on an area of activity close to the prize; this will usually be a specific topic or practice, and they will stay in that area to improve their chances of doing whatever tasks they deem useful or necessary to gain advancement. If the job is not secured or they have lost out, they will focus their attention in a completely different avenue to gain another prize. They will then move to that area, set up a temporary camp, and seek to position themselves in such a way as to increase their chances of success. They will repeat this behavior until they have won the prize.

The same logic can be used to seek patterns in your opponent's behavior in trying to eliminate competition in the workplace. They can move from location to location, set up a temporary camp, attack, and then move on once the threat has been removed. It can also, less sinisterly, apply to the movements of an employee attempting to learn about their environment, upskill themselves, or, essentially, receive information that is necessary to complete tasks.

An example of the levy flight foraging hypothesis applied to the corporate world is provided here with a generic everyday flowchart on page 102.

We are essentially looking for patterns and some sort of order within a volatile and unpredictable world to help us determine our own survival strategies.

This relates closely to another scientific mathematical theory, pioneered by French mathematician Henri Poincare in the early 20th century, known as "Chaos theory." This too seeks to establish how each activity leads to relationships and even seeks to interpret how small changes to a pattern of behavior will influence an entire system of interdependencies. While we will never know every single interaction and dependency of every complex process, we can seek to interpret likely scenarios and outcomes using the best information available to us.

An example of this is predicting the weather, which, although not an exact science owing to natural circumstances beyond our control, yields the best predictions on the basis of the evidence.

One aspect of chaos theory is the famous "Butterfly Effect," pioneered by mathematicians Edwards Lorenz and Henri Poincare in the late 19th

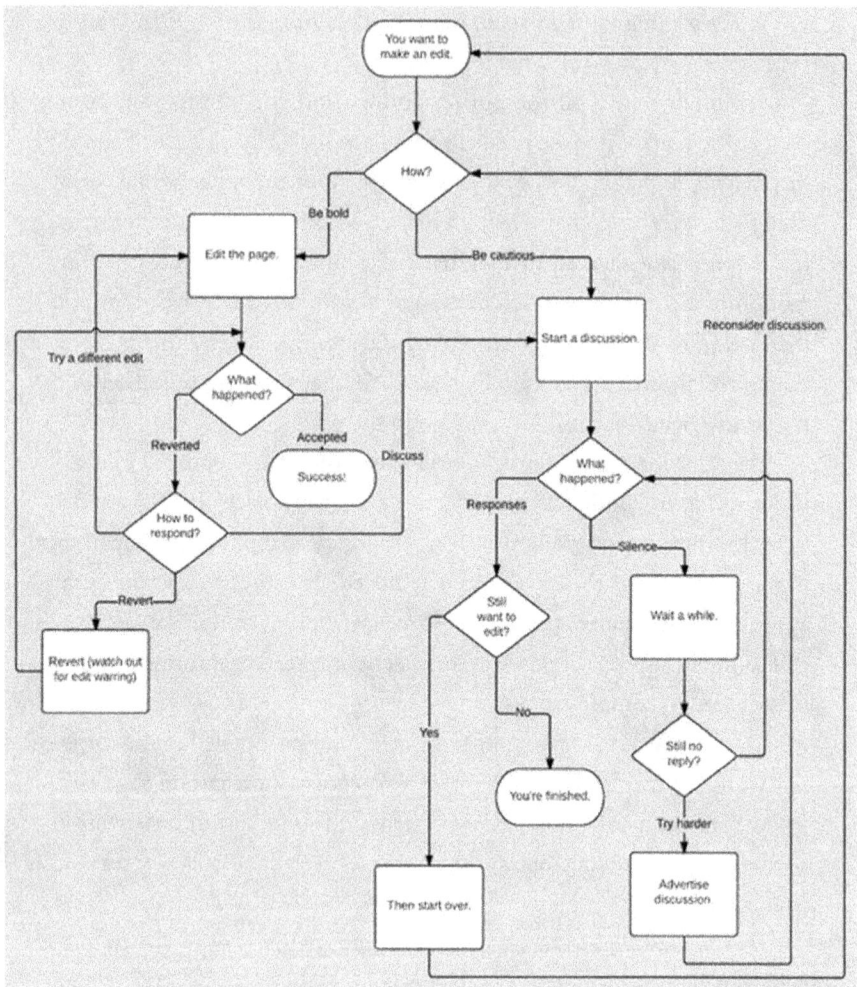

century, which uses the metaphor of a tornado's formation resulting directly from minor vibrations caused by the flutters of a butterfly's wings weeks earlier. This was used to explain how small seemingly inconsequential changes to data or conditions can change the overall course of a larger complex prediction of a weather system.

# CHAPTER 3

# Know Your Environment

*Natura non facit saltus*
*(Nature does not make jumps.)*
Gottfried Leibniz, German Philosopher 1646–1716

Having previously assessed your opponent within the corporate jungle, this chapter aims to take it a step further by undertaking an assessment of your specific corporate jungle and understanding how the organization's culture that presents on a daily basis intertwines with the animals that inhabit it.

When dealing with all animals within the corporate jungle, you will find that they normally fall into four distinct categories in regard to their performance and abilities:

1. **Unconsciously Adept**

   People in this category are coworkers and managers who do not know how effective or influential they actually are. This has both positives and negatives, in that this behavior can be exploited by others to achieve their self-serving goals, but, on the positive side, the worker will receive natural respect and admiration, allowing them to conduct operations more smoothly.

2. **Consciously Adept**

   People in this category are coworkers and managers who are aware of their positive impact and influence on others or the wider organization. Having this knowledge allows them to position themselves correctly in order to exploit others or certain opportunities that may arise. This knowledge or self-awareness, however, is not always used for nefarious purposes and can contribute to job satisfaction, because productivity and motivation will normally be higher in these individuals.

3. **Unconsciously Inept**

People in this category are coworkers and managers who are unaware of their limitations and inabilities and the negative impact that they have on others. They can cause a lot of damage to individuals and the organization as a whole if they are not identified and managed appropriately.

4. **Consciously Inept**

People in this category are coworkers and managers who are aware of their own inabilities and will seek to bluff their way and exploit others to ensure their survival. This is possibly the worst type of behavior, because you are dealing with a conscious entity who seeks to conceal themselves from you and others. We will look more at this type of person as we go along.

You must try and work out which category each of your opponents falls into through your everyday interactions, and you must be aware of opponents pretending to be in one category when they are actually in another.

## Unnatural Selection

To fully understand the corporate jungle, you must let go of the ideals of fairness and justice.

These two traits do not normally happen naturally, so you must always instigate their emergence.

Mutualism is a process that happens regularly in the wild jungles, relying on two or more different species interacting with each other to ensure their collective success. This can be done either consciously or unconsciously; an example of this process is birds sometimes landing on hoofed animals to prey on the ticks that inhabit their hides. The bird benefits from feeding on the food that is attracted to the hoofed animal, and the hoofed animal benefits from getting rid of an irritating insect that causes them discomfort.

The same behavior always tends to be replicated in the corporate environment, where animals will often rely on other animals to achieve their personal goals and objectives.

This can manifest itself in a consciously inept line manager relying solely on their subordinates to provide the work or output that they can ultimately extort and for which they take credit, but it can also lead to what can be termed unnatural selection.

In situations of "unnatural selection" within the corporate jungle, it usually results in an inferior species being selected for advancement or promotion by a more senior employee with the sole purpose of relying on shortcomings in that inferior candidate's personality or morality to ensure their own survival. This is why sometimes no matter how well you do in an interview or how much experience or qualifications you have for a role, it will not matter because the system can be rigged to ensure that the hiring manager's preferred candidate is successful in the interview.

Occurrences of "unnatural selection" are often difficult to spot for the uninitiated and will normally be realized only by other internal candidates, because external candidness will not have insight into the politics of a new environment necessary to make this assumption or discovery.

Subtle indications of unnatural selection can be identified however, if you pay close attention to the actual interview process. In situations where the process is rigged, you may not even be called to interview, but if you are you can easily spot this behavior by paying closer attention.

First, it must be pointed out that all interview panels normally have an HR representative and/or an independent panel member in order to ensure that corporate governance, fairness, and transparency is taking place. I am not suggesting that HR is aware of this behavior but merely stating that they can be led astray by the hiring manager through underhanded methods of choosing one candidate over the other. This is usually achieved through the use of the technical information discussed during the interview and is normally endemic to the hiring manager so they can sometimes be seen to be conversing with the candidate in a language that the HR professional or independent panel member does not understand.

A common tactic of unnatural selection by a corrupt hiring manager will always look to award the preferred candidate more points than the best candidate. In order to do this, multiple leading questions will be aimed at the preferred candidate in an attempt to nudge them into giving a more detailed example or hitting the correct buzzwords. Hence, if you have ever been in a situation where you are asked no questions in an interview by the panel, do not always assume that you have given the perfect answer. This process can often be spotted by experienced HR professionals, however, and is not endemic to all organizations.

In order to tip the scales back in your favor, however, you must finish every answer by asking the panel if there is any aspect of your answer that they would like you to clarify for them further in case you accidentally omitted any relevant information critical to the question asked. This can therefore hamper any potential favoritism because the hiring manager will no longer be able to use lack of information given as justification for awarding you a lower score.

When trying to get a handle on a specific corporation's culture, you must observe the behavior of those that dwell within it. Careful attention must be paid to specific behavior in relation to even the most basic of interactions, with break times or lunch times usually being an important opportunity to observe whether any cliques and instances of corporate mutualism are being displayed. You will see who speaks to whom and where they congregate. Over time patterns will emerge, and a profile of these interactions can be useful to note in relation to any future interactions that you may have with these individuals.

It is also important to observe the organization's demographic statistics, which can inform the culture also. The age group of your coworkers is also important to see how you fit in, because many age groups are threatened or put off by an age group that is younger or older to them. You must remember that a young office doesn't necessarily imply immaturity or indeed energy and that an older office doesn't always imply experience or even stubbornness. The issue arises when there is a specific concentration of demography that determines a specific culture in which the members become resistant and distrustful of change. A healthy mix is always the desire of all successful corporations.

In addition to the age profile, the diversity of species and their skillset that are present must also be observed to identify whether the correct animals are working in the correct environment. Are a team of rain forest white-tailed deer trying to scale the canopy layer, or is a parrot trying to navigate its way on the rain forest floor?

These facts will have a bearing on your own performance in that you will ultimately rely on these animals to complete objectives, so you must be able to work with them and see them as capable of helping you. If they are not equipped to help you, you must seek to find another place within the jungle to ensure your survival.

This naturally leads on to office territorialism, where many employees will have great affinity and pride within their work and will not take too kindly to new animals encroaching on their turf. You must seek to understand all instances of territorialism before you find yourself exposed in someone else's patch. Sometimes, however, it is necessary to take over someone else's territory, but you must be prepared to battle. To ensure your success you must establish the history or previous ways of working on all projects linked to this encroachment. This will then enable you to respond to any attacks that will ensue. The only way to win this battle is to be more knowledgeable than the current owner. Territorial gains must be swift and carried out with stealth and precision and have no emotion. An emotional response to the territorial gain will result in reprisal, and you will be seen as making it personal.

Cultural or local customs must also be observed and adhered to and will ultimately help you fit in with your new department. These local customs will not be apparent to you from the outset, and no one will actually make a point of telling you of their existence, because, normally, the locals perceive these customs as only natural, like breathing, and many would be unaware that you are not accustomed to some of these quirks.

A classic example I have of these customs dates back to when I first started working in England and normally made a cup of tea for myself in the morning and took it to my desk to drink while I looked at my e-mails. I was unaware that there was a system of "tea rounds" in operation, in which each member of the floor had the responsibility to make tea at different times of the day with an unwritten rota in place.

I was not observing established office protocol, so when I finally realized what was going on and eventually walked the length of the office floor to take a drinks order, I was quickly met with remarks of "Oh, I thought you would never ask."

Another important fact to observe is the rate of employee turnover within your department or wider organization. This can give you an indication of toxicity levels that are present or merely as an indicator of the future prospects of advancement within your field or specific area. Are you working in a stagnant pond, or is your role simply a stepping-stone to much greater things? Time alone will reveal this answer.

E-mail and phone call etiquette within a specific organization is also critical in ensuring survival.

Not returning e-mails or phone calls can frustrate everyone equally within all organizations, but care must be taken to adhere to the actual format and delivery of these communication staples within your specific organization.

Overly familiar terms such as referring to e-mail recipients as "folks" or "lads" are always a no-no, and care must be taken to address everyone as professionally as possible. Nor should you use short e-mails with information or instructions contained within the title bar. Also avoid the dreaded "FYI please see below" e-mails, where the sender does not take the time to summarize the issues or associated actions, forcing the recipient to scroll through large chains of information in order to make assumptions as to what the relevant actions actually are.

Phone call etiquette is equally of importance within the corporate jungle because you must not come across as insincere, aggressive, or overly superficial during conversations. Although politeness is necessary to convey sincerity, do not appear weak, but always strive to be assertive and honest within your conversations. People will appreciate this and remember these particulars as you must understand that all office correspondence, be it verbal, or e-mail related has a bearing on how you are perceived within the organization. Being too aggressive, as also being too passive, will always have a negative effect on your reputation and ultimate advancement.

You must also understand the dynamics of politics within your own team of direct reports if you are a line manager.

If you have replaced a respected predecessor, it will normally have resulted in a member (or multiple members) of your team having lost out on the opportunity for promotion, so there will always be that innate resentment to your appointment. If you have the luxury, however, of appointing your own team, this animosity will obviously be reduced, but you must remember that even your own team of direct reports, even if you are respected or liked by them, are also corporate animals who will look out for their own best interests, so never reveal too much to your own team: familiarity always breeds contempt. You must also remember that your own team of direct reports are not your friends but colleagues and that there must always be a line in the sand that must never be crossed. Once this line is crossed, productivity will decrease, as will your grip on authority and ultimate reputation.

Another aspect of corporate culture, and one closely related to cliques, is the occurrence of "out of hours" socializing. This is normally characterized by "after work drinks" or "nights out on the town." These can be extremely unnerving and somewhat dangerous events, however, because years of a person's good reputation and prestige can be essentially wiped out in one drunken night of uninhibited theatrics.

When alcohol is consumed you will normally lower your guard, and your true emotions and feelings can be discovered. Your disdain or admiration for various aspects of corporate life can be easily exposed, and you will have given your position away and left yourself vulnerable to many predators both known and unknown.

The trick here is to create a balance: You do not want to be seen as cold or uninterested in social interactions with your colleagues and peers, but you should not care too much as to give them your time when you do not want or need to be there.

You must remember that you are normally not friends with your co-workers in the true sense of the word "friend" as stated earlier; you are colleagues. You can be courteous and engage in lighthearted banter, but you do not know them well enough to let your guard down, and some corporate animals will use this as an opportunity to press you for information. You must realize that many office friendships are the result of bonding over negativity as people who gossip do so as a coping mechanism in such a way as to gain some semblance of control over a situation. Gossiping is a sort of release designed to let off some steam for the person who is under pressure or affected by a negative situation. The old phrase "misery loves company" is very fitting on these occasions.

These corporate "nights out" are often havens where office gossip and politics are discussed openly, so in some respects it is a toxic environment but is useful, nonetheless, to gain insights into the very inner workings of a team's dynamic. This, however, is not a sinister plot on your behalf, but merely an attempt to get a handle on the lie of the land without actually contributing. You must never feel pressured into revealing your thoughts on these occasions; simply just listen but not in an obvious way.

The ideal behavior is to attend the night out, drink sensibly, and leave before it gets to an unsociable hour. Never be the last to leave or the first to show up. Staying in the "goldilocks zone" will take time to master and is easier said than done, and you will usually have experienced the negative aspects of this endeavor at some point in your career.

Another closely linked instance of out-of-work socializing is technology based. Corporate colleagues are now more connected than ever before through social media platforms such as WhatsApp, Instagram, and Facebook. This online presence can attract corporate predators seeking to learn more about you in an attempt to figure you out. Having an outstanding "friend request" on Facebook from a colleague who is relatively unknown or not so much liked is always a testing time. Do you reject the invitation and incur the indignity of them knowing that you rejected their "friendship" request, or do you accept their invitation and invite them into your personal world, allowing them access to intimate information on your life? My advice on this issue is clear—simply do not accept invitations from work colleagues; there are a million more benefits to ignoring their invitations than there are to accepting them, but the main one is privacy. You may even consider using an alias when on social media to avoid any potentially unwanted invitations and help keep your private life hidden.

Group chats on WhatsApp follow the same principle because they can be seen as easy game for unwanted advances or interactions. You should not seek to block someone without reason but should always seek to enter "ghost or privacy modes," whereby they cannot see that you have read their messages.

The type of corporation will also have a bearing on the culture that is reflected. A large multinational company will normally have more diversity than a national or even local organization, but the size of the organization is immaterial, because more people do not necessarily mean more collaboration. On the contrary, larger spaces can mean more room for people to hide, and so the grass isn't always greener when contemplating a move to a larger organization in order to seek better productivity.

When effectively assessing or evaluating your environment, you must be aware of how the motivations of its inhabitants relate to the overall creation of the organizational culture.

When trying to make sense of this somewhat opaque environment, you must seek to understand the very fabric that enables the framework of this environment to function and how it shapes or is indeed shaped by its inhabitants. Successful outcomes within a competitive environment do not normally occur without interdependency or cooperation with others. This is true of all environments and is not just limited to the corporate world; the same principles also apply to the animal kingdom and to the battlefields, among others.

This is where the concept of game theory is best evaluated.

### Game Theory

The concept of game theory, although a subject of great study by many prominent scientists, was pioneered by scientists John von Neumann and John Nash in the late 19th and early 20th centuries and is essentially an attempt to apply mathematical modeling to determine the outcome of decisions or motivations made by each player.

Do not be confused, however, with the words "game" and "players", because this theory is applied to all sociopolitical, economic, military, and even evolutionary scenarios and concepts the world over and is seen as a key part of strategy formulation.

The game is essentially the dilemma, and the player can be a person, an organization, or even a country. Decisions are therefore "game moves" within each strategy that have a goal and are referred to as "payouts." These payouts can be shown as a number in a matrix.

The study focuses on the players, termed agents, and the strategies and interdependencies that are required to essentially make up the game. In order to "play the game" effectively, each agent must possess the ability to adapt and make choices or strategies based on information that they ultimately act on to affect the possibility of achieving their prize, or "payout," as it is known as.

The ability of the agent to make these choices effectively is referred to as possessing the "relevant agency", and the payout received is linked to the specific objective or goal that is their desire, which is referred to as their "value system".

The players are defined by their goal-oriented behavior, and in these games the players must interact with other players, with goals and payouts sometimes being shared.

Owing to the level of interaction required to successfully play these games, each action made by each agent or player will therefore positively or negatively affect the payout of another player.

In order to effectively model each game and predict the outcome, you must be able to define what value each agent desires the most.

In organizations all employees are agents, and the strategies they devise to play these games can be studied in order to determine behavior and motivation, as patterns can emerge each time these games are played. Why a coworker is fixated on a certain objective or course of action can be best explained by game theory principles.

When one finds oneself in a situation of conflict possibly because of competing agendas, game theory can best be used to explain the rationale and look at possible solutions.

The very premise of game theory relies on interdependencies between players, and each game can be characterized as being cooperative or noncooperative in nature. Understanding the difference between the two can assist you in determining the motivations or specific objectives of each player and how they will ultimately impact you.

## Cooperative and Noncooperative Games

In a nutshell, cooperative games involve agents working together to achieve a solution that is either shared or selfish in nature. A classic example here is that of a football team, where individuals work together to score goals and to defend against goals being scored against them with the ultimate aim of winning a trophy. Each player has a part to play, and success is outside the complete control of one person, because it depends on the actions of each performer, although it also has a collective element. Hence, cooperation is key to success.

Let's look at an example within the corporate world of cooperative games; this could take on the basis of a bonus structure, whereby if a team hits a collective target each person will receive an equal payout. This will promote cooperation, teamwork, and, ultimately, productivity.

Noncooperative games can either be by deliberate design or as a result of poor regulation and are present if the agents cannot form alliances or do not need to form alliances. Each player within these games is deemed to act in their own self-interest.

Some noncooperative games can be referred to as "zero sum" games because with only one possible winner, there is only one sum paid out to the winner, and therefore there is no incentive for cooperation.

A classic example of this is boxing, which has only two players; a team is not relied on for success because the actions of the individual alone are required in the overall success of the performance.

Noncooperative games involve both agents attempting to devise a strategy for optimizing their payout, and a natural balance arises when each player chooses to recognize the optimum strategy of their opponent; at this stage both agents are carrying out their best strategy. This way an outcome can be predicted. A "solution concept" is a prediction of your opponent's optimum strategy within a game.

This natural balance is referred to as an "equilibrium" and is essentially the point where each agent has figured out (assumed) what the other agent's strategy is. This phrase has been coined the "Nash equilibrium"; and each time that specific game is played, however, the more opportunities there are to spot patterns and predict outcomes.

A Nash equilibrium is achieved when each player uses their best possible strategy (known as their dominant strategy) while being aware of the available strategies of their opponent, and once the Nash equilibrium is achieved, there is really no need to change your strategy at this stage because you have chosen what you deem is the optimum strategy in line with your assumption of your opponent's dominant strategy in order to ensure an outcome that favors you and ensures your survival.

Let's look at a corporate example of noncooperative games and remain with the foregoing example of a team bonus. Let's just say now that the bonus structure has been removed by management with the structure now more commission based. This will promote the "every man and woman for themselves" attitude and may have a negative effect on overall team productivity as underhand tricks can now be utilized to achieve greater success with trust and teamwork being diluted.

A classic example of an interdependency game that is noncooperative can be seen within the famous prisoner's dilemma, where cooperation and competition are both evaluated by both players in order to make a decision that will benefit the individual.

## Prisoner's Dilemma

Two employees, Chris and Gavin, have just been arrested for their roles in a fraud case. There is evidence to convict them both for embezzlement, with each due to receive a minimum of 10 years in jail for their roles. Police also suspect that one of the men committed security fraud as part of the process to assist with the embezzlement, which if proven, will result in an extra 5 years being added to one of their sentences.

Both men would have been aware of the details of the security fraud but only one was required to carry it out, but police do not have sufficient evidence to determine who it was.

The police place the two perpetrators in two separate interview rooms. The prisoners cannot communicate with each other, so they are said to possess 'imperfect information' but as soon as both prisoners are offered the same deal and are made aware of this fact (common knowledge) they also know the consequences of each choice (complete, but not full, information).

The police require only one confession from the two perpetrators as to who was responsible for the security fraud, but neither man will ever confess to being the ringleader.

The police therefore give Chris the following options:

- an additional 5 years in jail (on top of the original 10 for embezzlement) if he stays silent and **does not** testify against Gavin but Gavin **testifies against him**; total—**15 years in total**
- 10 years in jail if he stays silent and **does not** testify against Gavin and Gavin stays silent and **does not** testify against him; total—**10 years in total**
- if **both testify** against each other, 2 more years are added on to both their initial 10 years sentences; total—**12 years in total**

The police make the same deal to Gavin:

- an additional 5 years in jail (on top of the original 10 for embezzlement) if he stays silent and **does not** testify against Chris but Chris **testifies against him**; total—**15 years in total**
- 10 years in jail if he stays silent and **does not** testify against Chris and Chris stays silent and **does not** testify against him; total—**10 years in total**
- if **both testify** against each other, 2 more years are added on to both their initial 10 years sentences; total—**12 years in total**

The most appropriate outcome for both parties is for none of them to testify against the other but to remain silent because they will receive the minimum punishment of 10 years in jail. (Co-operate) The risks, however, are excessive, because each prisoner will now be naturally suspicious of the other and seek to protect their own interest. This will result in each of the prisoners opting to blame the other (defecting) because this is deemed to have the lowest risk in the absence of all the information. This is not the best outcome for both prisoners, but a Nash equilibrium has been achieved.

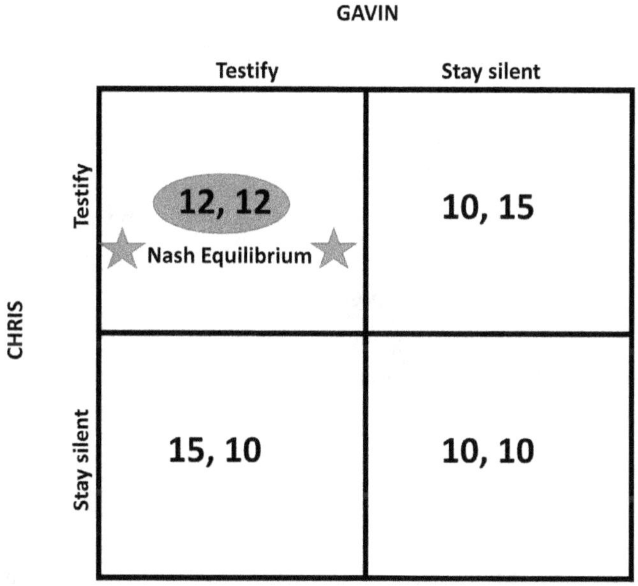

GAVIN

|  | Testify | Stay silent |
|---|---|---|
| Testify | 12, 12 (Nash Equilibrium) | 10, 15 |
| Stay silent | 15, 10 | 10, 10 |

(CHRIS on left axis)

Figure 3.1

As you can see, the Nash equilibrium is not necessarily the best outcome and is made only by individuals to ensure the survival of each individual player (utility maximization). It does not usually have the best outcome for a group, but the Nash equilibrium can therefore be used to predict the results of similar games.

Noncooperative games can also arise through poor regulation in the absence of a third party to promote cooperation; competition and conflict will therefore be present. This is because laws and policy promote cooperation as each player will be aware of the consequence of the other playing unfairly.

The payouts to your opponent must be understood so that you can determine how they may formulate their strategies. These can be ranked either in order of importance, which is referred to as "ordinal ranking," or when one specific determined payout is deemed to exist this is referred to as the "cardinal payoff."

When looking to understand motivation and better your outcome in any corporate encounter, you must have a view of the limitation of your opponent as well as yourself. In scenarios where a departmental promotion is hotly contested between you and others, how badly do you and your opponents want that promotion, and to what lengths are you both willing to go to achieve it?

This where you look to what are known as "minimax" and "maximin" strategies.

A strategy designed to produce an outcome that causes the least possible damage or conflict to you is called a minimax strategy. Players will therefore often look to seek out their opponent's minimax value as well as their own.

A maximin strategy is an attempt to gain the highest payload, and opting for such a strategy exposes a person to the highest risk despite being fully aware of the consequences.

Let's now look at how noncooperative games can affect the wider organization.

## Social Dilemma

Noncooperative games can produce what is called a "social dilemma." This is where the individual is motivated to put their own self-interest before the larger team, because higher payouts can be achieved by selfish choices made to better their own self-interests and rewards. Sometimes, to combat this an organization will try to promote the teamwork ethos and look to promote more shared rewards.

This, however, can also have its difficulties. One such difficulty relates to the emergence of what are termed "public good games," where the individual benefits from the collective actions of others but does nothing to assist in the process.

Let's take the first example again of a collective team bonus given to all employees. If a department achieves its overall target, this can promote teamwork and raise overall productively, but what if not all of the players are pulling their weight and the prospect of doing nothing will still provide them with the same rewards as those received by their colleagues who do all the work?

This, unfortunately, is just human nature, so organizations should seek to strike a balance.

The answer to solving social dilemma situations and winning 'public good games' is regulation.

Let's take the example of a water company issuing a hosepipe ban in the middle of an unusually hot and dry summer, in a city whose population is told to conserve water. One citizen, however, chooses to ignore the instruction, feeling that their contribution alone is paltry and will not make a difference and therefore relies on the rest of the population to comply. But what if everyone had that attitude? Well, the reservoirs would be depleted and there would be no water.

Hence, a way to combat this is in the form of regulation. There must be consequences for individuals that do not comply. This can be done by placing individual water meters at every house to determine usage and fine those who are deemed excessive users. Another method to combat this is via incentivization.

We can use the example of reducing carbon footprint, by heavily taxing fossil fuelled vechicles and a subsidy scheme rolled out as an incentive to buyers to go electric.

So to assist in this shift away from self-serving strategies, organizations must seek to communicative effectively with all employees and link their individual performance objectives to shared goals. This results in the creation of interdependencies and highlights to the individual the significance of their individual role in ensuring the collective success of the team or the wider organization.

It is therefore imperative that organizations that wish to increase productivity must seek to regulate individual competition and promote an altruistic form of teamwork.

## Evolutionary Game Theory

This is a continuation of game theory applied to populations within the animal kingdom.

It was pioneered in 1973 by scientist John Maynard Smith in an attempt to best predict the strategies of competing animals.

It has been used to best explain the element of cooperation in the animal kingdom and how to produce the maximum results for the population. It goes a step further than this and theorizes that successful animals will pass other successful traits to their offspring, thereby ensuring the survival of the entire species.

The main game that Maynard Smyth analyzed was the one referred to as "Hawk Dove."

A player can be either a Hawk or a Dove but does not reveal which animal he or she is at the outset.

The strategy of the Hawk is to display aggression, which can escalate into a fight with another Hawk in which they either win or lose. The dove can also be aggressive but retreats when challenged by a Hawk but does not display aggression when facing another dove, so the prize is shared.

Hawk meets Dove—Hawk Wins (50 percent chance of Hawk encountering Dove)

Hawk meets Hawk—50 percent chance of winning

Dove meets Hawk—Hawk Wins

Dove meets Dove—Both share (50 percent chance of Dove encountering another Dove)

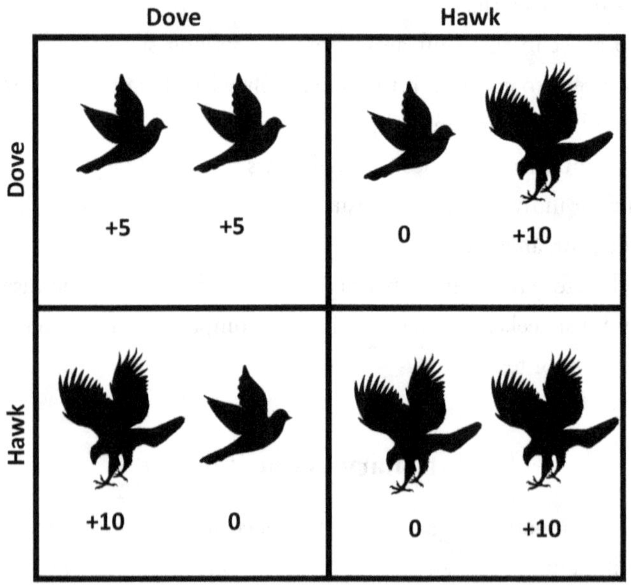

Figure 3.2

The benefits to both players of not displaying aggression can be seen as the best statistical outcome for both.

The foregoing game is described as pure competition because there are no elements of sociability to be taken into consideration. Maynard theorizes that when sociability is present there are factors that must be taken into consideration to inform the optimum strategy. These include cooperation, spite, selfishness, and altruism (selfless concern for others) and can be displayed in the following example:

When seeking to explain this, I will summarize this in an everyday office setting:

Jane and Mark are strong candidates for a promotion at work but are aware that there is only one position to be filled. Their manager advises that two presentations are due to be presented at the end of the quarter on both their areas and that the more impactful of the two will determine who will be in pole position. Regardless of who gets the role, if both presentations go well, the entire department will receive an increase in budget and other associated benefits. They both, however, need to cooperate in order to gain the relevant information from each other so as to be able to complete both their individual reports.

Although both employees would prefer not to have a meeting together to gain this information from the other because they will be revealing their work strategies to their competitor, they realize that if they do not, neither of them will have the information necessary for their presentations and the department will suffer. When in a meeting to discuss information sharing, Mark becomes aware that Jane's presentation looks much better than his, and the thought of sabotage crosses his mind, that is, to give Jane the wrong information to complete her presentation. If he sabotages her presentation however, the entire department will suffer; he then contemplates giving her the correct information because in doing so the entire department will benefit. Seeing how well Jane's presentation looks, Mark also considers giving the information honestly because he knows that she deserves to win. The thought of fair competition also crosses his mind, the motive being to see who the best really is.

There are thus four options:

- Do not have a meeting to exchange information (Selfishness)
- Sabotage the information when giving to the other player (Spite)

- Give the information to benefit the entire organization (Cooperation)
- Give the information to help the other person to the greatest extent possible (Altruism)

Let's see how this plays out in a matrix.

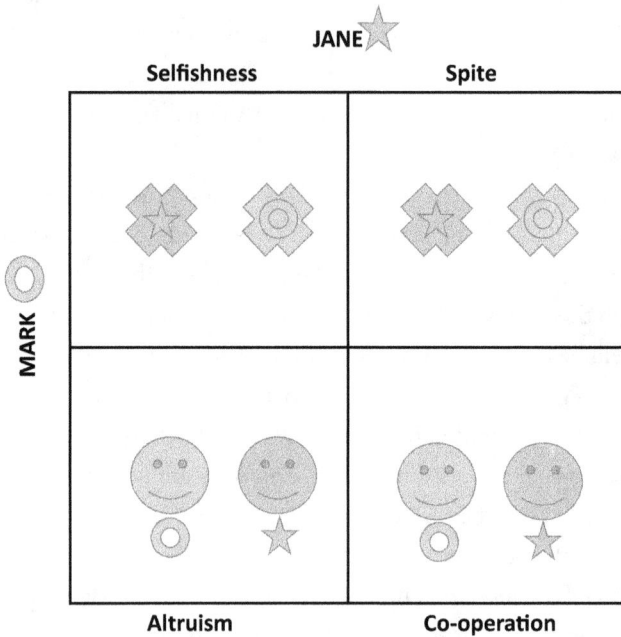

*Figure 3.3*

If Mark either cooperates naturally or is altruistic, it will have a benefit for the whole department (including Mark) despite Jane receiving the greater prize. This highlights the benefits of cooperation in the workplace.

# CHAPTER 4

# Know Yourself

*Vincit qui se vincit*
*(He conquers who conquers himself.)*
Publilius Syrus, Latin Writer born in Syria (85–43 BC)

Let's now look at how you fit into this wild world.

In order to survive in the corporate jungle, in addition to knowing your opponents and your environment, you must also know yourself.

To do this effectively, first try and see what animal you identify with the most, because possessing similar or conflicting traits will naturally draw you toward or repel you from certain behaviors or attributes.

Let's look at an academic study, undertaken in 1983 by researchers Kidd, Kelley, and Kidd, in which they matched companion animals to owners' personality types to ascertain the physical and psychosocial benefits. The study, entitled "Personality Characteristics of Horse, Turtle, Snake, and Bird Owners," revealed some interesting results:

*Tests showed that the horse owners were assertive and introspective but low in warmth and nurturance. Male horse owners were aggressive and dominant while female horse owners were easy-going and non-aggressive. Turtle owners were hard-working, reliable, and upwardly mobile. Snake owners were unconventional and novelty-seeking. Bird owners were socially outgoing and expressive. Like male horse owners, female bird owners were high in dominance.*

Another study was carried out by Professor Richard Wiseman, from the University of Herefordshire, in which 2,500 people submitted online questionnaires about their pets.

Owners of various pets were asked questions about how they view their pets in relation to traits such as intelligence, happiness, independence, and sense of humor. He discovered that pets and their owners over time displayed similar characteristics, just as married couples mirror each other after long periods of being together.

Another study, by Sadahiko Nakajima, a psychologist at Japan's Kwansei Gakuin University, undertook a study in 2009 to determine whether humans and their pets look alike.

His research revealed that people were able to match dogs with their owners correctly by looking at photographs of their faces with various obstructions. In pictures where the eyes were visible, 80 percent of the 500 participants correctly matched the owner to their dog. When the eyes of either the owner or the dog were obstructed, there was zero accuracy. This revealed that people sought out pet dogs that looked similar to themselves.

My take on this is that humans will ultimately try and anthropomorphize animals and seek out pets that remind them of themselves, that they can identify with and fit into their lifestyle. This could be narcissism, selfishness, or simply an instinct that we carried through evolution.

All this information may explain why we are drawn to certain types of species in the office or why we are repelled by many because they are essentially incompatible with our own emotional makeup.

If we put this in context, that animals mirror their owners and vice versa, how does this affect the corporate world? First, let's look at what types of animals are most prevalent in society:

The 2019–2020 APPA (American Pet Products Association) National Pet Owners' survey revealed how many US households had which pets: The results showed that 63.4 m households had dogs, 42.7 m had cats, 11.5 m had freshwater fish, 5.7 m had birds, 5.4 m had small animals, 4.4 m had reptiles, 1.6 m had saltwater fish, and 1.6 m households had horses.

This information, coupled with the fact that 157 million people made up the US workforce in 2019, shows the diversity of the corporate jungle.

## Before Entering the Jungle

You must compare entry into the corporate jungle every morning to the way a soldier enters a battle or a boxer enters the ring; you must be prepared.

Preparation in this environment is very much linked to your sleep and morning routines, because if they are not in balance you will be ill prepared to spend a day in the office.

Sleep deprivation or lack of food will not work in your favor, and despite your best efforts in repelling or defending attacks, you will not be on your "A–game," so you must ensure you are well slept and well fed before starting the day.

Your journey to work also influences your stress levels, because if you are constantly rushing to be on time, your stress levels will be out of balance before you reach your desk. Being late also has repercussions, and opponents will always observe this and use it to their advantage, so you must strive not to score own goals in relation to timekeeping. Please always remember to keep a tidy workstation, because having an untidy one implies a disorganized demeanor to your opponents and will be seen as a vulnerability. A desk should always be treated as a base, so you must ensure that you have it protected at all times and that you do not leave valuable information unattended.

You must also be aware of dress codes and etiquette so as not to stand out unnecessarily. You do not need any unwanted attention because you must seek to blend into your environment as much as possible. Any attempts at looking to stand out signal the pursuit of validation, which is not warranted through work attire. Any other alterations of fashion such as revealing outfits or bling accessories should also be avoided. You must appear the consummate professional, and your work attire should be viewed as a combat uniform, so it must be practical.

We have already discussed in Chapter 2 how an imbalanced ego can lead to issues with certain people and the impact that it has on their personalities, but you must be aware that your own ego may also be imbalanced. An imbalance doesn't always lead to trouble, but it can create unrealistic perceptions and traits that you expect either of yourself or from others.

An imbalanced ego may be attributable to your nurture, that is, always being told that you are right or, possibly, that you are always wrong, and you therefore strive for validation in every encounter you find yourself in.

You can also have confidence or self-esteem issues that manifest themselves as aggression in order to deflect from the actual issue or, conversely, you could exhibit a high level of shyness and find it hard to interact or face conflict in any way.

Balancing the ego is the only way to deal with these situations in a normal environment, but you must be aware that corporate offices are not normal environments and that, therefore, an imbalanced ego (or perceived imbalanced ego) can also be a defense mechanism, so do not always view it as negative.

How can an imbalanced ego be positive or even a defense mechanism? I'm sure you're wondering, "Well… it's all about optics."

To put it bluntly, the corporate world, despite all its successes and prestige, as we have seen earlier, is essentially a game.

It is a game in which you wear a costume with your corporate attire and you try and advance to the next level via promotion. In a game you must use tools to assist in your quest, and these tools are purely psychological. This may be the Machiavellian part in me coming to the surface, but you must understand that if you do not realize or accept that you are in a game, others do, so regardless of your belief, you must be aware of the realities of all these encounters.

It is important to note that although it is a game, it doesn't detract in any way from the moralities that are present, because many corporations do wonderful things for society and the environment. The 'game' label, as we have discussed in the previous chapter, refers to the interactions and interdependences, and the title merely denotes the strategies that people employ to survive within it. The same relates to war; where there are war games, the 'game' label does not detract from the seriousness or horrors that war presents, but merely suggests that a strategic element is present.

How many times have you heard the phrase "just play the game" mentioned in the office? A good few times I would imagine.

Hence, as stated earlier, the tools used in this game are psychological in nature, so if you are a meek, mild-mannered, loyal upstanding member of society in real life, this persona can have both positive and negative impacts on your interactions with others in the workplace. For example, people may seek to test you and take advantage of your good nature to fulfil self-serving agendas, so there is a chance that you can be 'played like a fiddle' and not even realize. So how does one stop this? Well, the first step is to create a persona, one that highlights to a predator that you are dangerous and not to be messed with. (This aspect is discussed in greater detail in Chapter 5—Warfare)

Appearing to have an imbalanced ego will therefore make potential attackers less likely to attack, but sometimes opponents may also seek to exploit this perceived persona that you are displaying in order to bait you into reacting in a certain way; however, if this is not your real persona, their efforts will be in vain and will not adversely affect you. (Baiting is also covered in greater detail in Chapter 5—Warfare)

## Instinct versus Learned Behaviors

Let's now look at how instinct plays a part in surviving the corporate jungle. Instinct is defined by the *Cambridge English Dictionary* as follows:

*The way people or animals naturally react or behave, without having to think or learn about it*

So it's clear that instinct is a naturally present element of your behavior that you cannot learn; you are born with it. Just as a frog knows how to swim or a lizard seeks out the shade, it cannot be an unnatural forced behavior; it is very much imprinted within the subconscious psyche.

But you must understand that instinct can have both positive and negative aspects.

You've often heard the phase "trust your instinct," which directs a person to trust their gut feeling within a certain situation. This can therefore steer the person to listen to their own feeling and natural interpretations to react to a certain situation. Instinct is therefore very much related to survival.

But what if your instinct tells you to run away when you know that you need to stay and fight. This is perceived as being the negative or indeed less helpful part of instinct.

In order to break the cycle and experience growth, you must seek to sometimes defy or overcome natural instinct and turn to 'learned behaviour.'

Learned behavior is essentially a mechanism that you have adopted to deal with situations that are deemed outside of your comfort zone. This is always associated with risk but is the only way a repetitive cycle of fearful instinct can be broken. What are the ways or overcoming natural instinct when it is seen as an inhibitor of growth, I hear you ask? Well, the most effective way is through a conditioning process called 'Systematic Desensitization.'

## Systematic Desensitization

This is a therapy created by South African psychiatrist Joseph Wolf in the 1950s, which essentially tries to decrease your fear of an object or an encounter by simply controlling your exposure to it.

Your exposure is incremental and contained, starting from low exposure to medium and working up to full exposure over a period of time so you can handle the fear aspect at lower doses, therefore increase immunity and desensitization, and work your way up to full desensitization,

An example of this would be that a person who had a fear of dogs would be constantly exposed to a low dose of doggy company, starting with observing the dog from a safe location, then working up to feeding the dog in the presence of a handler, and then after they became accustomed to this, encouraged to pet the dog in the presence of others. From then onward, with each step, the fear is gradually reduced, until the person feels comfortable taking the dog for a walk without handlers. Therefore, the instinct to be fearful of dogs has been overcome by learned behavior.

This now leads to an aspect of human psychology, whereby we are reluctant to readily prepare to relinquish our instincts in order to replace them with new learned behavior. This may be attributable to an internal battle that you are having with yourself over ethics or even a refusal to believe that a reality is actually taking place. This is what is known as 'cognitive dissonance.'

## Cognitive Dissonance

Cognitive dissonance is a theory proposed by American psychologist Leon Festinger, in the 1950s, positing that when a person holds two or more contradictory beliefs or values or acts against one of them, they will encounter psychological stress. He theorizes that this is a response to not accepting new information that is not deemed natural to them.

So cognitive dissonance can be compared to a crisis of conscience that you may have when new information is presented to you that you find hard to believe or accept.

This crisis of conscience will most likely present various defense mechanisms within you as you try and make sense of the reality that you are being presented.

Sigmund Freud defined many of defence mechanisms:

Let us look, however, at the ones most pertinent to everyday corporate life.

# Denial

When you first enter the corporate jungle, you will immediately realize that it is a far cry from the safe haven of school or college. The literature and study materials will not always equip you with the prerequisites necessary for survival. These traits must be learned and adapted in order to ensure your survival. Sometimes, however, accepting or adapting to this new reality will invoke a sense of denial in your conscious psyche. I am not suggesting that anything immoral is taking place but merely stating that practices or procedures that you will find yourself undertaking may be the antithesis of what you actually perceived yourself doing when you dreamed of this role as a child.

For example, you spend years studying to be a lawyer, graduate at the top of your class, and during the first day in the new role you find yourself being told to make tea for everyone or instructed to carry out frivolous tasks such as photocopying, but you somehow convince yourself that this behavior is acceptable and that it will get better over time.

# Repression

Repression takes denial a step further by mentally shutting out information that is deemed harmful or a tragic experience that you may have witnessed or experienced. This is the defense mechanism, where the brain chemically overrides the natural response to react.

# Stockholm Syndrome

This occurs when you identify with your captor or attacker and become sympathetic and protective towards them or their cause.

This happens when someone has been brainwashed by a manipulative force or chooses to irrationally express these feelings by their own free will.

## Displacement

This is a process whereby a response or retaliation that should really have been aimed at the attacker is now aimed at someone else instead. A classic example of this is your manager roaring at you and you, in turn, roaring at your own direct report.

## Reaction Formation

This is the process whereby you portray a reaction or emotion that is not your characteristic natural response. You may choose to appear fine and content on the outside, having witnessed wrongdoing or something that made you uncomfortable, but you appear calm, collected, and unfazed on the outside.

All these defense mechanisms must be realized if you are to interpret your own natural responses to conflict and understand how you will need to adapt in order to overcome them.

This section of the book, as discussed earlier, is to make you aware of your own strengths and limitations so that you can be aware of how you could be impacted when entering the corporate jungle. There are, however, other human factors that you must realize in order to successfully negotiate the corporate jungle terrain.

## Stress

Stress is the main killer within the corporate jungle environment.

According to a study carried out by Oregon State University and published in the *Journal of Experimental Gerontology*, people who perceive their lives to be stressful were three times more likely to die than those who did not perceive their lives to be stressful.

Caroline Alwin, director of the 'Centre for Health Aging Research,' who led the study at the university, explained that

*There are a number of ways that chronic stress can kill you, that in-cludes increased levels of cortisol levels that interfere with learning memory, lower immune function and bone density and increased blood pressure, cholesterol and heart disease.*

Another study, published in the *British Medical Journal,* in 2012, stated that even low levels of stress or anxiety can increase the risk of fatal heart attacks or strokes by up to a fifth. This is based on a study of 68,000 adults over an 8-year period.

Stress can therefore be linked to every major health problem, so your exposure to stress must be monitored and reviewed.

Exposure to stress, however, is sometimes unavoidable, and I have recently seen studies in which people maintain that low levels of stress can be a good thing as they encourage a productive response. I can believe that stress can produce a productive response in many situations, but we have clearly seen in the foregoing that exposure to long-term low levels of stress can decrease our life expectancy by a fifth. It doesn't seem such a good thing now.

Only you can gauge your exposure and ultimate reaction to stress, but, as stated previously, it will affect your cognitive abilities in situations where you rely on them the most.

As we have also seen earlier, the stress hormone cortisol, when pro-duced, can cause serious negative effects both physically and mentally. There are also more well-known stress hormones released in battle, called adrenaline, that essentially release blood flow to the muscles and heart and that form our natural fight or flight mode. This can have a nega-tive impact on physical and mental health, but sometimes we cannot avoid these situations that we find ourselves in, where we will exhibit our automatic responses or our newly learned behaviors. You must also be aware that adrenaline can affect your ability to concentrate or focus because you are essentially blinkered by fear or rage in addition to a plethora of other emotions. (We will discuss the fight vs. flight mode in Chapter 5—Warfare.)

One final thing to remember on the topic of stress is that you must never be too prideful or independent to ask for help. All battles are won through the assistance of allies, and "no man or woman is an island," so you should never see it as a weakness to ask for assistance when times are overwhelming. Not seeking assistance shows an imbalanced ego, which is a dangerous condition to have in any stressful situation.

## The Importance of Compasses

When traversing all uncertain terrain and environments, it is important to always have a handle on your bearings. A way of keeping track of this in the jungle is via a compass, which shows you the way to magnetic north each time you are lost in order to keep you on track.

The metaphorical compass used in the corporate world is actually a part of your life outside work, be it a partner or a child, a mother, father, sibling, pet, or even a cause or sport that you are part of—essentially any factor that reminds you of what life is all about and stops you losing yourself in the corporate environment. If you do not have a compass, it is more likely that you will be consumed by your environment and your ultimate view of reality will be distorted. The phrase "unable to see the wood for the trees" rings very true here. You must also be aware of the influence that the corporate jungle is having on your life outside work.

## Success and Enemies

Throughout this book you will see references to both opponents and enemies; the distinction being made is that having enemies implies having a baggage in an encounter, whereas having opponents does not.

Having this baggage with an enemy can therefore reduce your maneuverability and therefore effectiveness in any given situation, so the inference here is that no one should consciously seek to unnecessarily create enemies for themselves because of the negative effects it can have on your overall performance. It is an inevitability, however, that enemies will be present despite your best efforts and can actually have benefits, as we will see as the book develops.

It is also important to understand that opponents don't always become enemies, so expending an unnecessary amount of energy or emotions on your opponents isn't always warranted.

The point also rings true that you should never unnecessarily reveal yourself to your enemy where possible, because staying hidden will always go in your favor.

## Respect

*A feeling of admiration that you have for someone because of their personal qualities, their achievements or their status, and that you show by treating them in a polite and kind way.*

www.Macmilliandictionary.com

It is very important to receive a sense of respect in your role as it will always stand in your favor and make life much easier. Respect, as the old saying goes, is a "two-way street," because to receive respect you must be seen to be giving it. Respect can be achieved via two methods:

1. **Respect by admiration**

   This is when a coworker recognizes your achievements or capacity and acknowledges this to you via their conduct and behavior. You must be aware that this acknowledgment may often only be subtle and displayed by your opponent in a passive natural form.

2. **Respect by fear**

   This type of respect is not achieved passively or naturally; it is sought via aggression and fear. It conveys the consequences to your opponent of not overtly respecting you. This is not a true form of respect, and the behaviors exhibited by your opponents toward you will differ from those behaviors enacted behind your back.

   It is therefore imperative that you seek respect the hard way; that is a form of respect that is actually merited.

The constant pursuit of respect should be natural and flow smoothly in order for it to be effective to your progression within the corporate world. You must also be aware of the fine line between respect and an imbalanced ego, because the constant pursuit of respect can highlight the pursuit of validation of your behavior and success, which actually highlights a vulnerability within you.

You must understand that respect is not a yardstick for success but merely an enabler to achieve it.

## Ambition

*An ardent desire for rank, fame, or power.*

www.merriam-webster.com

Having ambition is definitely not a bad attribute. It shows that you are motivated, and sometimes ambition is the driver to getting out of certain situations in life where you feel trapped or whereby you feel that you have learned all you can at a specific level in an organization and wish to progress and develop.

You may also seek to gain more money to buy a house, car, or start a family or anything else requiring money. Ambition in this regard is therefore healthy. It can give us hope and lead to the feeling of overall high motivation and excitement.

Too much ambition, however, can be a bad thing because it will consume each working day and, if not achieved in line with your own personal objectives and timelines, may lead to self-loathing, negativity, and the creation of insecurities.

You must realize that being the most intelligent or experienced member of an organization does not always imply automatic progression. There may be instances when you are hard to promote because you are deemed too good at your job and others who are left to pick up the pieces may be deemed by management as being not as capable as you. This is what I refer to as 'corporate pigeonholing,' a leading cause of staff turnover in all organizations.

You must also realize that the system can be rigged to allow for artificial selection at the hands of self-serving senior management who have their own agenda, so you should not be so naive as to think that hard work and success within your role will automatically lead to progression. Therefore, make your plans only after you have made a careful audit of your specific corporate environment.

You must also learn that in the cooperate jungle, no matter how indispensable you think you are or try to make yourself, there is a law that always applies to our tenure, and that is that we are all replaceable. As harsh as that sounds, you must learn that every human being in the corporate world has a replacement waiting in the wings, whether seen or unseen, that can take over our role and pick up the pieces required to keep the organization afloat.

Human beings outside the corporate world are not replaceable however, as we are fathers, mothers, daughters, sons, friends, and family. Once you process and accept this fact, only then will you find peace in your daily interactions and interdependences.

You must also be aware that seeking to remain at a particular level of management within the corporate world for too long is not advisable. Guerrillas must keep moving to be unseen, just as a shark must keep moving or it will die, and, therefore, staying longer in a camp is always fraught with danger.

It is much harder to hit a moving target, so you must be wary of becoming stationary and of the implications of the increased level of visibility that this will bring upon you. I'm not suggesting that everyone must not stop pursuing promotion until they are awarded the position of CEO, because that would not be feasible, there being only one such position; what I am saying, rather, is that once you stop moving, the level of attacks on you by your opponents will increase, so you must be prepared to fortify your base. Once you reach department head level, it is much easier to remain in position owing to your authoritative position with the organization, but in 'middle management' it is much harder to remain stationary without incurring further attacks, because everyone coming up the ranks wants 'a shot at the title' and will be out to prove themselves. Staying too long in one position will also pigeonhole you and lower your chances of promotion. Sometimes when you can't move up, it's better to move sideways; what I'm suggesting here is to increase your skill set by taking on a new challenge in another department via a transfer or secondment; this makes you more adaptable, and the experience that you will gain will benefit you somewhere and sometime, possibly even in another organization.

**Life is like riding a bicycle; to keep your balance you must keep moving.**

—Albert Einstein

# CHAPTER 5

# Warfare

*Si vis pacem para bellum*
*(If you want peace, prepare for war.)*
Publius Flavius Vegetius Renatus, Roman Writer, 4th century BC

In this chapter of the book we are entering the combat phase. Corporate combat can take many forms, and, as you will soon see, battles are not normally won or lost on a traditional battlefield, but away from prying eyes and normally do not result in a single drop of blood or sweat being spilled.

During the research phase of this book, and indeed having an interest in the psychological effects of war, I have meticulously researched the great military leaders of both the recent and the very distant past.

The environment and maneuverability issues within the terrain presented make guerrilla warfare the only effective method of corporate combat.

It does not rely on numbers to ensure strength and advantage but, rather, being lower in numbers, aids maneuverability. It relies solely on stealth and passion.

The most important literature on all war stratagems is the book *The Art of War*, by Sun Tzu.

This manual, written in the 5th century BC, continues to inform modern military strategy to this very day. The main points within the book espouse the importance of knowing yourself and your enemy before any wartime interaction, but the most powerful message that resonates as being the most succinct in all instances of combat is the following quote:

*The supreme art of war is to subdue the enemy without fighting...*
*therefore the skilful leader subdues his enemy's troops without any*

*fighting, he captures their cities without laying siege to them, he overthrows their kingdom without lengthy operations in the field... Hence to fight and conquer in all your battles is not supreme excellence; supreme excellence consists in breaking the enemy's resistance without fighting*

The principle here is to fight only when absolutely necessary and to use psychological means rather than physical combat.

You must also understand that many human beings are naturally reluctant to battle, and numerous wartime studies have examined in depth the behavior of combatants who are reluctant to fire on or engage the enemy, a fact that is of significant interest to military leaders and strategists. We will look at these instances further on in this chapter.

## Corporate Psychological Warfare

In relation to corporate psychological warfare, however, it is important to understand how your corporate opponents behave under stress or in conflict situations in order to best understand how to successfully exploit their weaknesses and win psychological battles.

Throughout my career I have observed an array of key natural behaviors exhibited by employees that I feel effectively inform any stressful encounter or threat of conflict within the workplace. Humans will ultimate move into one or all of these seven layers in every encounter where conflict is envisaged or presented.

Seven responses to corporate stress and conflict:

1. Retreat
2. Freeze
3. Deflect (deflecting blame or responsibility or getting others to fight your battles)
4. Surrender
5. Deception
6. Deter (active and passive threats)
7. Fight

1. **Retreat**

This is essentially the "fight or flight mode," where the combatant is so overwhelmed by the prospect of battle or stress that they retreat in haste. They either do not wish to enter combat because they will either feel completely inept or, if possessing significant strength, will ultimately realize that they are not as strong as their opponent.

In the corporate world, an opponent usually retreats when they feel inferior to your intellect or knowledge in a given situation. It will normally result in territory gain by the protagonist.

Fleeing will also manifest itself by an employee going "off the grid," unable to be found in times of pressure.

Let's look at the science behind fleeing.

*In response to acute stress, the body's sympathetic nervous system is activated due to the sudden release of hormones. The sympathetic nervous system stimulates the adrenal glands triggering the release of catecholamines, which include adrenaline and non-adrenaline. This results in an increase in heart rate, blood pressure and breathing rate.*

www.verywellmind.com

Fleeing the scene is also an adaptation of survival in the wild, in that animals can ensure their survival to "live and fight another day," and is used as a tactic within guerrilla warfare to ensure the survival of the guerrilla to inflict attacks in the future as they are concentrating more on the war and not on the immediate battle.

*There is in all this (retreat), it would appear, a negative quality, an attitude of retreat, of avoiding frontal fights. However, this is consequent upon the general strategy of guerrilla warfare, which is the same in its ultimate end as in any warfare: to win, to annihilate the enemy. Thus, it is clear that guerrilla warfare is a phase that does not in itself afford opportunities to arrive at complete victory. It is one of the initial phases of warfare and will develop continuously...*

Ernesto "Che" Guevara—Guerrilla Warfare

## 2. Freeze

*He who is not afraid of death by a thousand cuts dares to unhorse the emperor.*

Mao Tse Tung

When a person instinctively freezes, they are unable to function at all. They are consumed by fear or shock owing to the stress of the situation and are essentially incapacitated for quite some time.

Let's look at the science behind freezing:

*For the first time, neuroscientists at the University of Bristol have identified a brain pathway that may be the root of the universal response to freeze in place when we are afraid. Their revolutionary study, released on April 23, 2014, discovered a chain of neural connections stemming from the cerebellum. When activated by a real or imagined threatening stimuli, these neural connections can cause the body to automatically freeze.*

www.psychologytoday.com

Freezing in battle renders you and your team helpless and therefore vulnerable. The methods to overcome freezing are to use the techniques that we covered in Chapter 4 on systematic desensitization. You must prepare yourself to experience the fight or flight hormones.

Overcoming fear is the only way to avoid freezing.

Another aspect of freezing is Hesitancy:

*The worst calamities that befall an army arise from hesitation*

**Sun Tzu—The Art of War**

Let's look at the definition of hesitation:

*If you are hesitant, you do not do something immediately or quickly because you are nervous or not certain.*

**Cambridge English Dictionary**

In times of conflict many people hesitate as a way of coping with or attempting to process the stress. It is extremely important to scrutinize all aspects related to an issue before making a decision, but constant overthinking implies a lack of courage when faced with all the necessary information to make that decision. It is a natural instinct to attempt to cover all the bases, but it can show a weakness to your opponents.

Prolonged hesitancy is not a positive attribute and will result in issues being delayed because decisions are unable to be made by those who are required to make them. It is often the result of deep-rooted insecurities held by the hesitant person.

Hesitation is a dangerous flaw in a combat situation because it will, more often than not, leave you exposed, reflecting as it does a lack of self-confidence and conviction, which are necessary in all combat situations.

Another subsection of Freezing is Procrastination.

Let's look at the description of Procrastination from **mindtools.com**

*Procrastination usually involves ignoring an unpleasant, but likely more important task in favour of one that is more enjoyable or easier.* So what is the science behind procrastination?

*Procrastination boils down to a battle between the limbic system and the prefrontal cortex. The limbic system is a set of brain structures containing the pleasure centre, while the prefrontal cortex controls planning and decision making. The prefrontal cortex is less developed and thus weaker, so often times the limbic system wins out, leading to procrastination.*

—UPMC Department of Neurosurgery

When someone procrastinates in the corporate world, it can have both direct and indirect consequences for all stakeholders. If a person tasked with delivering a key project milestone starts to procrastinate because of the stress, it may be hard to actually see how much damage has been done before it's too late. They will then look to deflect the blame. Managing procrastinators, however, doesn't require micromanagement techniques; it simply requires check-in meetings with those who hold key responsibilities. Some people, however, leave things till the last minute, seeming to enjoy the adrenaline rush that the stress brings. It is not an ideal attribute, but as long as the work is done correctly and on time, let them have their 'fun' without, however, allowing their behavior to add stress to other people in the team. If leaving tasks to the last minute negatively impacts on others, the procrastinating behavior must be called out immediately.

You can see the negative effects that procrastination and hesitancy can have on your performance and how it can be detrimental to your survival in the corporate jungle.

### 3. Deflect (deflecting blame, responsibility; or getting others to fight your battles)

*The best weapon against the enemy is another enemy.*

**Friedrich Nietzsche (Austrian Philosopher)**

The act of deflecting is a common occurrence in stressful situations. It involves the threatened party either shifting the blame to another colleague or actually nominating another colleague to fight their battles or undertake their responsibilities. Deflection is a cowardly act because the deflector will throw another colleague under the bus in times of stress and can even be cowardly enough to use their stronger allies in an attempt to scare you off.

Another aspect of deflection is known as 'psychological deflection,' which is actually linked to narcissism, in which the protagonist refuses to acknowledge their mistakes and will always seek to shift the blame onto someone else rather than admit their own faults. Consequently, people who constantly deflect blame will, ultimately, never develop on a personal level.

### 4. Surrender

This is the most straightforward of reactions, because it normally involves admission and truth from the surrendered party. They simply admit that they cannot undertake a specific task, citing inability, time constraints, or some other reason. It contrasts with fleeing in that it involves a keener sense of self- awareness and admission.

Surrendering is not always a negative attribute because, although it can cause havoc in the middle of a project if a team member surrenders, owing to stress, it can also have a positive effect if the member concerned gives up at the very outset of the task so that they can be substituted to keep the project on track.

Other aspects of surrender happen when either you or another person refuses to engage the other in battle in view of the perceived losses potentially being incurred in battle after you have weighed all your options. This aspect of surrender, like all other aspects of this categorization, involve a keen sense of self-awareness.

The key, however, is to force your opponent into surrender before the battle begins; we will see how this is done in the next section—Deception

## 5. Deception

*All war is based on deception…Hence, when able to attack, we must seem unable; when using our forces, we must seem inactive; when we are near, we must make our enemy believe that we are far away; when far away, we must make him believe we are near.*

**Sun Tzu—The Art of War**

This reaction is undoubtedly the most effective and efficient way to deal with conflict.

Sun Tzu attributes the success of all warfare to deceptive techniques. Let us look to our study of our opponents to best assist in the development of these necessary techniques:

As we have learned in Chapter 2, animals adapt in many ways to escape predators or attract prey. This can take many forms, so let's start with a process known as "mimicry," in which you mimic a certain style or character to increase your chances of survival.

Mimicry is of four distinct types:

### I. Aggressive Mimicry

This is when a predator mimics a less harmful species to avoid detection in order to increase its hunting success. Otherwise known as the "wolf in sheep's clothing" approach, it is a common tactic used in the corporate world as many opponents will often conceal their true intentions and appear to gain your trust as a way to infiltrate your territory.

In the corporate world this is very obvious, as a potential aggressor will mask themselves to you initially in order to gain your trust, but once they have you in a vulnerable position they will strike.

Instinct is very important here, because, although trusting your natural inclinations will give you an advantage in identifying the attacker, sometimes learned behavior is required to successfully defeat them. You must learn to be suspicious of flattery, overt displays of commendation, sympathy, and empathy because these can simply be tools the enemy uses as a lure to gain your trust.

## II. Batesian Mimicry

This process, named after British naturalist Henry Walter Bates, occurs when a harmless animal evolves to imitate the warnings or characteristics of a harmful species in order to deter predators.

A classic example of this in the jungle is between the poisonous coral snake and the harmless king snake. The coral snake, being poisonous, is avoided by predators, which see the warnings of the distinctive coloration that they have learned to avoid; this is then replicated by the king snake, which has adapted to possessing the same red and black banding coloration to deter predators.

Corporate Batesian mimicry manifests itself in exactly the same way. This is when a person learns behavior or skills from a coworker that are effective in fending off predators. This could relate to observations on how a person speaks or behaves in order to deal positively with or avoid conflict.

In order to accomplish successful Batesian mimicry, however, it will require a keen understanding and profiling of your environment and its inhabitants. Batesian mimicry in the wild has taken some time to adapt and gain success, so do not be discouraged if these methods do not work the first time.

This process in the corporate world is essentially where a vulnerable or exposed species mimics the action of another to portray competence or success. This is, essentially, a form of bluffing or embellishment of one's abilities.

An example of this could be as extremely simple as observing a colleague in your new environment resisting the daily approaches of a pushy stakeholder by creating a weekly meeting or report where all concerns are addressed. This allows them not to be pestered on a daily basis and gives them time to collate a response, or it can extend to more complicated occurrences, as when you observe a colleague invoke a specific contractual clause on an aggressive client or customer in order to deter their unproductive behaviors or pursuit of unwarranted commercial demands.

### III.  **Mullerian Mimicry**

This process, named after German naturalist Fritz Muller, takes place when one toxic animal seeks to mimic the appearance of another toxic animal that has been successful in deterring predators with the goal of using the successful species' success as a form of shared protection.

In Mullerian mimicry, one species relies on the already established success of the other species as a way of gaining the same level of avoidance from their shared predator. A predator may have to learn to avoid the new species' toxicity, which will take time and result in many attacks in the process to gain this key information, so the prey merely speeds up the predator's learning process by mimicking traits that the predator will naturally avoid, thereby ensuring the prey's survival.

This is mirrored in the corporate world, where an experienced or highly intellectual employee who was well regarded in the previous organization has just started in a new organization and has not yet established themselves as a leader in the new company because they are essentially unknown.

The reputation that they held in their previous organization was key to their success in that they were able to perform tasks quickly and efficiently because everyone knew who they were and always trusted their opinions or gave them a "wide berth" in many or all situations.

So in order to speed up the process of recognition and respect in their new organization, they simply seek to mirror the actions and behaviors of already established leaders currently within the organization in an attempt to be viewed in the same light by all in the organization, ultimately securing a passage to better productivity.

### IV. **Calls and False Alarms**

Mimicry can also assume the form of calls made by predators imitating less threatening animals or even mimicking the prey itself.

This is done to trick prey into believing that the threat is not severe, as in the case of the Margay cat mimicking Tamarin monkeys in the Amazon rain forest to attract them to their demise.

Conversely, it can also be used by prey to imitate predators to trick them into thinking that they possess a much greater threat than possible, or it can simply be done to trick competitors who are competing for the same food sources. The fork-tailed Drongo, indigenous to the Kalahari, has been recorded making false alarm calls of predators such as hawks in order to trick their rivals into dropping food or to move them away from potential food sources.

In the corporate world this behaviour is carried out via learned vocabulary and business buzzwords spoken to make a person appear more intelligent than they actually are. You will learn however that not everyone who talks in buzzwords is a bluffer and not everyone with a 'well spoken' accent is intelligent.

False alarms within corporations usually take the form of disinformation. Disinformation can essentially spread fear among stakeholders and have both positive and negative effects on productivity. You must therefore question the authenticity of all information and learn to distinguish fact from rumor. I am not suggesting a distrustful attitude toward every piece of information received, but only highlighting the need to be aware of the source and the facts before making your next move. Do not ever base any action on faith alone, because disinformation is usually spread for a reason that can sometimes be nefarious or part of a colleague's self-serving agenda.

## Baiting

Baiting in the animal kingdom involves using food or a desirable environment to draw in prey, such as the presence of meat or fruit, and will normally be tailored to the specific animal being lured.

Baiting in the corporate world, however, is very different, involving psychologically taunting or goading someone into exhibiting a desired response. This response is usually anger or frustration, and it can be used as a tactic in many corporations on a daily basis.

Baiting within the corporate world can wear many guises. It can be the prospect or promise of a promotion or pay rise that makes you jump through hoops but that never materializes, or it can be identified project shortcuts that appear to positively influence your critical path or increase your productivity.

Any unofficial promises of promotion or pay rises must always be approached with caution. You must ask yourself why you are being given this information.

In giving you this information the informant wishes to gain something from the transaction in return.

Most promotions or advancements that are genuine do not involve the release of this information to the employee beforehand, although you may have received indications, without ever being told outright.

You must always treat all talk of advancement with caution because it may simply be used to get you to work harder or faster or take on more responsibilities, with the advancement never materializing.

The second aspect of baiting involves perceived shortcuts in projects or quick productivity wins. These must also be approached with extreme caution because they may just be attempts to lure you into a trap set by unscrupulous colleagues or stakeholders who have a vested interest in your failure. All shortcuts must be carefully examined before being used, with full attention paid to all potential consequences.

The third element of baiting is associated with behavior. This is where a colleague or stakeholder wishes to provoke a response from you in order to 'show you up' in front of stakeholders or senior management. You must learn to spot these techniques used because they will more than likely evoke comments designed to undermine your confidence or abilities. They will usually follow patterns such as "I thought you would have known this" or "this is what happens when you don't plan things properly."

These are normally designed to evoke feelings of humiliation or aggression.

Our earlier discussion on the benefits of a perceived unbalanced ego can also be applied quite successfully to baiting. Here, the attacker, trying to provoke a response from you, is creating their strategy based solely on their interpretation of your personality, which is essentially the personality that you have chosen to display but may not be your true personality.

For example, you may actually be a very self-confident capable employee but downplay your confidence or abilities in certain aspects of your work life. This is done to expose enemies because when they seek to knock your self-confidence, you will not be fazed and they will be easily exposed.

# Camouflage

Camouflage is a technique effectively used in warfare and also by animals in the wild to avoid enemies and stalk prey, so it can be ideally suited to corporate environments too. Camouflage is essentially the passive or active act of concealment and is characterized by the following five categories.

### I.  Background Color Matching (Passive and Active)

This method of concealment involves a single background into which an animal can blend owing to its natural coloring. It also results in guerrillas choosing the correct attire when in combat situations—green clothing for jungle and khaki uniforms for desert warfare.

Passive background matching implies an unconscious or natural adaptation of concealment against a background over time. An example of this in the jungle is tree snakes disguising themselves against the foliage of the canopy.

Active color background matching, although still a natural adaptation, implies more of conscious effort to conceal oneself against a background that is not your natural portrayal or resting state.

An example of this in the wild is the orange Oakleaf butterfly or dead leaf butterfly, which resembles a leaf when its wings are closed in a state of rest to evade predators.

In the corporate world this method of concealment is utilized both consciously and subconsciously to ensure you are doing all you can not to stand out from the crowd.

Passive color matching takes place when an employee cannot be differentiated from their peers or project teams because they are all seen as high performers with the natural abilities required to carry out their role. They all have the required education and expertise and possess the specific skill set necessary to ensure success in the task that they are undertaking. This is a natural adaptation in that the employee has educated and adapted themselves to be in this position and is capable of performing.

The converse of this example is also true, because all of the team just referred to could be equally inefficient and unproductive, with no single employee being identifiable as being more unproductive than anyone else. It therefore ensures the survival of the individual within a group.

Active color matching, however, is when one or more employee does not have the required skill set or abilities required to perform a certain task but makes it appear that they do.

This is a form of bluffing because the employee is essentially a passenger in the team and will appear to the naked eye as being equally as capable as the rest of the team. They may, however, still actually be as skilled as the rest but choose not to provide the same output for various reasons, e.g., laziness.

Active color matching is very hard to expose because it can be revealed only with individual targets that can sometimes hamper the collective moral and ultimate progression of a team's working capabilities. Individual targets may create a sense of interproject competition that will ultimately affect the productivity and output of the team's overall task. The reality of life is that active color matchers are usually present within all teams and projects, so rather than trying to beat or expose them, it's better to just learn to identify and avoid them where possible.

## II. Disruptive Coloration

This method of concealment involves an animal or guerrilla using patterns and designs to break up their outline against a background of different colors and hues. These patterns are normally characterized as stripes or spots and also assist in the movement of the animal/guerrilla against these different colored backgrounds.

Disruptive coloration within the corporate world differs from background color matching in that BCM is related solely to a specific project or task, whereas disruptive coloration is related to an employee's daily movement within all aspects of corporate life. It is effectively their persona, it is how they portray their presence in all situations, and it can be both positive and negative.

Disruptive coloration allows the employee to better blend into all environments when on the move. It allows them not to stand out unnecessarily and therefore not to reveal too much about their intentions or expose themselves. It is essentially their natural shield. The negative aspect, however, is that employees who possess these colorations are seen as 'Teflon' and cannot be held responsible for their actions within a given situation.

### III.  Countershading (Thayer's Law)

This is a method of concealment pioneered by American naturalist Abbott Handerson Thayer. It allows animals to better blend into their surroundings by masking their outlines against multiple backdrops. It is characterized by an animal having a lighter colored underside and a darker colored topside to avoid detection.

A classic example of this is best displayed in sharks in that their lighter colored underside, when viewed by prey swimming beneath them against a bright sunlit backdrop, can make the shark appear transparent and their darker top half, when viewed from above, blends in with the darkness of the ocean depths, making them less vulnerable to orcas or fishermen.

Corporate countershading is most common within middle management and involves a manager simultaneously concealing their intentions to their employees below them and also to their senior managers above them through deceptive techniques. They thus make themselves unaccountable because they cannot be held responsible for tasks that have gone awry, but they can choose to reveal themselves in times of praise to bask in glory.

## IV. Self-Decoration

This method of concealment involves animals or soldiers using natural items within the environment as props to better blend into their surroundings. An example of this in the wild is when decorator crabs disguise themselves with stones, seaweed, and mud in an attempt to remain hidden from predators or undertake 'lie in wait' techniques to catch prey. This is also characterized in military operations by soldiers wearing "Ghillie suits" to better blend into their surroundings.

Corporate self-decoration relates to membership of professional associations and achievements of educational qualifications.

These certificates are adorned and presented like war medals and are used to blend in with intellectual counterparts but sometimes can be used to repel potential attackers through intimidation.

## V. Motion Dazzle

Motion dazzle is the process of using carefully adapted patterns to appear subsumed by your surroundings while moving in order to make it difficult to be differentiated and "singled out" by a predator.

This makes it impossible for a cheetah to focus on an individual zebra in a herd during a chase because it sees them all as an undifferentiated mass of white and black.

Corporate motion dazzle is different from disruptive coloration in that disruptive coloration only refers to an individual employee's attempts at concealment against their surroundings when moving, whereas motion dazzle implies that the employee moves in a herd and conceals themselves within that herd when moving. Motion dazzle is also different from active and passive color matching in that active and passive color matching is normally carried out only in a static environment,

Therefore, corporate motion dazzle deals with a group of employees moving in a herd, affording them protection from the fact that they cannot be easily differentiated from one another. Examples of this are when a close-knit and highly productive team naturally cover for each other when a mistake has been made to protect the interests of the overall team. This is a passive form of camouflage and does not require any active consideration on their part as they are naturally a high-performing loyal team.

## Infrasound and Ultrasound

Infrasound is characterized by low-frequency sounds that are beyond the realm of what's deemed normal human hearing (20–20,000 Hz).

These inaudible sounds, lower than 20 Hz, however, instill a sense of disorientation, unexplained fear, and nausea.

Ultrasounds are, conversely, characterized by high-frequency sounds above 20,000 Hz. They have been adapted and harnessed in medical technologies to be quite useful, but beyond these utilizations any prolonged ultrasonic exposure can also have severe effects on human health.

Infrasound is used by various animals in the wild to communicate over long distances; examples include elephants, as we have seen in the previous chapter, but this select group of users also includes animals such as tigers and crocodiles and some species of birds such as peacocks.

The use of infrasound is an adaptation that animals use to assist their survival; in elephants the sound of distant thunder can lead them to a water source, and infrasound used by tigers can be used to threaten rivals and mark out territories.

Ultrasonic sounds are also used by animals in the wild and are most commonly used as echolocation to source prey and navigate their environment; such sounds are used by bats and whales.

Corporate infrasound and ultrasound deal with communication between employees that cannot be easily heard, identified, or deciphered. It can take on the guise of subtle expressions or words that say one thing but actually have hidden meanings to them. Infrasound is a defense mechanism that employees use to communicate with each other, mainly when around management. They give each other signals and signs via their speech that indicate or highlight to each other a possible course of dangerous action and to beware of certain pitfalls.

Long-range corporate infrasound can be carried out via e-mails or phone calls containing specially recognized code words or phrases to convey the information that a possible threat is near.

The historic warfare equivalent of infrasound is known as the bush telegraph, where drum sounds or smoke signals are sent to each other over long distances. The modern equivalent is solders talking in code over radios to convey specific information to each other about the enemies' location or any other specific objective.

## False Retreats

False retreats are exactly how they sound. This is where an opponent tricks you into thinking that they have retreated, only to lie in wait until your guard has been lowered in order to gain the upper hand via a surprise attack. False retreats can really be effectively identified by quickly evaluating your enemies' motive in relation to the retreat. You must realize who has the best firepower or strength. If it is you, then you can usually accept the rationale for retreat, but if you are evenly matched you must also question their motive for retreat and always be on your guard for reprisals. You must also always seek to pursue the enemy to ensure that retreat is genuine.

> When the enemy advances we retreat; the enemy camps we harass; the enemy tires; we attack; the enemy retreats; we pursue

**Mao Zedong**

## False Movements and Decoys

False movements and decoys are used regularly in guerrilla warfare as an attempt to focus your opponent's attention on one place when you attack from another. This can be in the form of strategically placed wires attached to buses or branches to indicate your false presence.

Corporate false movements and decoys essentially involve focusing the attention of stakeholders on one issue so that you can effectively deal with another issue in parallel.

Other examples, however, include an employee focusing your attention on one area in order to gain the upper hand and exploit or sabotage your efforts in another area, so you must always be aware of the motive when someone strongly suggests a course of action or dwells too much on a specific issue.

## Trapping (Flypaper Theory)

Trapping has been in existence since the beginning of time, and, in Chapter 2, we discussed its benefits in exposing opponents in the corporate world.

The trapping I refer to here, however, refers more to the magnetism of your opponent. The flypaper theory, coined by U.S. General Ricardo

Sanchez in relation to the Iraq War, intimates that taking the war to the enemy territory essentially focuses insurgency attention exclusively on the invading force, thereby leaving the innocent population alone back in the United States.

The corporate equivalent of this deals with the physical relocation of your activities and the psychological effects that result. For example, if you wish to engage an opponent who you feel is potentially trying to sabotage your work or project, you seek to take the fight to them, essentially focusing their attention on the fight at hand and away from their initial goal.

# Gaslighting

*Gaslighting, an elaborate and insidious technique of deception and psychological manipulation, usually practiced by a single deceiver or "Gaslighter", on a single victim over an extended period. Its effect is to gradually undermine the victim's confidence in his own ability to distinguish truth from falsehood, right from wrong, or reality from appearance, thereby rendering him pathologically dependent on the Gaslighter in his thinking or feelings*

**Encyclopaedia Britannica**

Gaslighting is one of the deadliest psychological methods used in the corporate jungle and can be more dangerous for new entrants into the office who are yet to work out friend from foe.

The only way to reduce the effects of gaslighting is to never depend on anyone to guide you. Only you are in control. Once you relinquish control and appear vulnerable to others, you are at the mercy of gaslighters who will prey on your weaknesses to fulfil their own self-serving agendas.

## 6. Deter: (Subsection of Deception)

Technically, deterrence falls within the area of deception, but I felt that it warrants its own specific subsection.

When engaging in guerrilla warfare, it is important to realize that traveling light is always the preferred course of action; heavy equipment slows you down and reduces your effectiveness and overall maneuverability. Guerrilla combatants throughout history have opted to mirror the weapons used by their opponents in order to rely on their opponents as their source of ammunition supply once the opponents have been disposed of.

One of the main protocols of guerrilla warfare is to use ammunition effectively, avoiding unnecessary waste, and aim strategically when firing, with ammo conservation given the highest priority. This protocol is not followed in conventional warfare by large regular infantry because battalions are usually bankrolled by extremely wealthy governments with large defense budgets.

Let's look at, for example, the war in Iraq. A report published in 2010 by the U.S. General Accounting Office (GAO) revealed that U.S. forces in Iraq and Afghanistan during the war on terror used 1.8 billion rounds of small arms ammunition per year, totaling $250,000 for every insurgent killed. An FOI request by the *Daily Mirror* also revealed that the British army in Afghanistan fired 46 million bullets over the 8-year war, firing an average of 10,000 per day and costing £200 million.

These facts do not point to any shortcomings on the part of the soldiers in relation to accuracy and do not attribute this rate to any strategic prowess displayed by the insurgents; they simply reveal aspects of the complicated area of combat psychology.

It can be argued that awareness of unlimited finance was essentially the reason for these rates of fire versus kill count, but this is not the case.

The reasons, I believe, fall into three categories:

A)  Strategic deterrents
B)  Operational tactics
C)  Natural reluctance to kill

## Strategic Deterrents

The U.S. military during the Iraq and Afghanistan wars, possessed state-of-the art weaponry that far surpassed its opponents' arsenals. This fact was well known even before the war started, because it is obvious that a superpower would possess the best equipment, but the effect of this must be fully understood. First, having better weaponry not only gives you a physical advantage but also gives the holder a psychological advantage over their opponent. Your opponent is less likely to underestimate you if you're using top-of-the line firepower. Simply firing off a few rounds in the general direction of your opponent with technically advanced equipment is enough to stop them in their tracks and suspend their advances. This will allow you time to regroup and plan your next move.

## Operational Tactics

Firing in the general direction of your opponent can also be used in operational tactics in order to flush out or move your opponents into a position of your choice. This can be to a location where you have better cover or they have poorer cover or can simply involve flushing your opponent out of an area and into an ambush by another unit of your team. So when firing your weapons, accuracy of kill shot is not always necessary.

## Natural Reluctance to Kill

Human beings are capable of committing multitudes of horrendous acts, but we are not born monsters; although we can debate the nature versus nurture aspect of human psychology until the cows come home, no human being, logically, wants to ever kill another. To be sure, there are instances of emotion or passion that result in murder, but it is a different kind of human being who likes killing routinely, a person who is biologically or chemically imbalanced.

The psychological impacts of killing will have a lifelong effect on the perpetrator—this is what separates us from the animals—so why would someone want to bring this burden upon themselves unnecessarily?

'Killology' was developed by combat historian S.L.A. Marshall, who discovered, by researching World War II and the Vietnam War statistics, that soldiers intentionally aimed and fired to miss the enemy. This fact is studied intensely by military strategists and analysts and is the main reason why military inductions are so strict and rigid. They are breaking you down to build you up into a machine, to desensitize you to the horrors of war.

You must remember, however, that soldiers are not machines and that despite all the propaganda and the medals awarded to soldiers, many of these 'machines' find it difficult to settle back into normal society after these periods of service duty.

In June 2010, a report commissioned by the U.S. Department of Defense's Pharmacoeconomic Center revealed that 20 percent of the 1.1 million active duty troops that they surveyed were taking some form of psychotropic drug to combat the effects of battle.

All of these points only reinforce the fact that we are not machines, but human beings reluctant to kill. There are always exceptions however.

The effects of deterrence are critical to all conflict situations. Having your enemy retreat or surrender is always the preferred outcome, because, as you must understand, fighting is usually the last resort within the corporate world.

The above facts reinforce the point that fighting will always be the last option in any natural conflict. When I say, 'natural conflict,' I do not include the man-made wars, as the soldiers fighting do not do so out of passion but because it is their job. It is better to get to the position that you do not have to fight.

To understand this concept further, let us first define the action of fighting. Fighting in the workplace and fighting on the battlefield are two separate and distinct processes. The former being exclusively psychological in nature, fighting is characterized by trickery, illusions, manipulation, and other psychological aspects in order to achieve goals rather than by physical force or restraint.

### I.  Honest Signaling (Passive)

Honest signaling in the animal kingdom is exactly how it sounds; it is an active display of behaviors or traits from potential prey in order to deter a predator from advancing.

Examples of this include behavior in white-tailed deer; when they sense they are being observed by jaguar, they exhibit a behavior known as 'stotting': jumping high in the air, raising all four legs as a display of physical fitness to deter a chase from the jaguar, signaling to the jaguar that the chase will not be worth it because the deer will be able to outmaneuver it.

Other examples in the animal kingdom of honest signaling are birds signaling to a predator who has been discovered advancing toward them in stealth mode. This signal, usually a call, signals to the predator that it has been roused and that the jig is up, implying that they should no longer waste their time in a futile attempt to stalk them.

Corporate deimatic behavior can appear subtle owing to the professional nature of the environment and can sometimes be overlooked, but do not be fooled, because it can equally have the same effect that it has in actual warfare. This behavior can take many forms that signal to the attacker to think twice about approaching you. This can be either active or passive in nature.

Let's looks at the example of a criminal attempting to mug someone on the street. Are they more likely to attempt to approach a muscle-bound man or a frail elderly pensioner? The physical strength exhibited by the strong man deters the attacker from attacking and therefore deflects their focus onto the weaker pensioner perceived as being more vulnerable.

Using the same example, let's imagine that the pensioner is being followed by the attacker and that the attacker realizes that he is actually out walking with his Rottweiler dog that is off the lead and appears menacing. How will this reflect on their perceived vulnerability now to the potential attacker?

This is exactly how corporate deimatic behavior works, because you are seen to naturally possess some set of protective armor that makes you appear less vulnerable to potential predators. This could be being a member of the union or having good relationships with key stakeholders, so if you are attacked it would have grave consequences for the attacker's reputation.

### Aposematism (Passive)

In the animal kingdom aposematic deterrents are very similar to honest signaling in that they are usually passive in nature, relating to the physical characteristics of the animal rather than a consciously active behavioral trait.

The process essentially involves animals displaying to predators a marking or coloration on their skin to highlight their toxicity to potential predators. Examples of this include the aforementioned golden poison dart frog and the corn snake's red and black circular pigmentation bands.

## II. **Deimatic Behavior**

The foregoing example of strategic deterrents in relation to ammunition superiority aren't the only examples of effective deterrence. As a natural rule, all displays of aggression are a form of deterrence in a conflict situation. The aggressor uses this self-assumed prowess as a threat, either veiled or apparent, in order to warn you of the consequences of engaging further. In the animal kingdom aggressive displays are a way of life to fend off threats and secure territory, and in the corporate world this is no different.

Deimatic behavior therefore differs from honest signaling in that these tactics are more conscious rather than subconscious. The foregoing examples concerning physical fitness being a deterrent to the attacker are passive in nature, in that the muscle-bound man didn't specifically do anything to deter the attacker, the strong appearance being just his natural physique.

The pensioner out taking his dog for a walk can also be a passive way to deter the criminal in that the pensioner in this example did not specifically procure this dog in order to deter attackers

Hence, we now turn our attention to the active signaling that can happen in these situations.

Let's imagine that the strong man in the foregoing example wasn't always a strong man and was continually picked on for his small or weak stature, so he spent years in the gym perfecting his physique in order to show others that he is not to be messed with. The example of the pensioner with the Rottweiler can also be explored further; let's pretend that the dog was obtained because of feelings of insecurity that the pensioner may have had owing to a potential shortcoming in his physical fitness or strength, so he uses the dog for protection. In this context the signaling becomes active rather than passive, conscious rather than subconscious and therefore moves from honest signaling into the realms of deimatic behavior.

In the corporate world, deimatic behavior can take the form of shouting and other aggressive displays and even veiled threats to deter you from pursuing a specific course of action.

You must realize that when someone shouts, they have essentially revealed a weakness within themselves because they have allowed stress or emotion to overtake their cognitive abilities. It is a sign that they are losing control.

### III.  **Playing Dead**

Playing dead is a technique used to great effect within the animal kingdom as a predator deterrent. As predators are mainly interested only in catching live prey, the thrill of the hunt can be more alluring than the prize. Playing dead takes the fun out of the hunt or chase, and predators will not normally prey on dead animals, so this technique has been adapted by many animals to assist in their survival.

The corporate equivalent of playing dead corresponds to playing down the benefits to the predator of attacking you. Why would a corporate predator expend unnecessary energy and risk reputational damage in pursuing a course of action that will have no benefit to them? Examples of this include not revealing success too early and always keeping information controlled and restricted to only those required to receive it.

### 7.  **Fight**

This category of behavior is normally utilized only when all the preceding six options have been assessed or expended. Engaging in battle is essentially the last resort in all areas of conflict.

But what about those people who are quick- tempered and can be aggressive, I hear you say? But you must understand that displays of temper and aggression are not true battles, as we have noted earlier; they are merely precursors to battle and a form of deflection or deterrent, merely tactics used to avoid battle.

As stated earlier, fighting in the workplace is completely different than fighting on the battlefield, for obvious reasons, but the same methodology still applies.

Corporate combat is exclusively psychological in nature rather than physical, and fighting happens when you actively pursue an employee or group of employees with the objective of engaging them in an attacking or defensive manner.

Fighting in the office always has the goals of exposing or vilifying the opponent and revealing them to others as being in a vulnerable state. This is done to advance self-serving agendas where you are seen as competition to your opponent for a coveted resource or position of advancement.

# Prebattle Considerations

When considering combat strategies, a plethora of information must be considered and evaluated beforehand in order to ensure the most successful outcome. In all conflict encounters the question of whether or not a battle is required or even worth it must be considered.

Are you essentially using a cannon to kill a mosquito, or are you bringing a knife to a gunfight?

You must also be able to establish the gravity of the situation beforehand and establish whether winning the conflict can be achieved through minimal or zero losses, because the consequences of incurring very heavy losses on your side will outweigh the benefits of winning. This is what is known as a 'Pyrrhic victory,' where the losses incurred by one side in winning are so severe that it is not a true victory, leaving you in a worse situation afterwards.

The type of weapons and amount of ammunition at your disposal will either positively or negatively influence your effectiveness.

You must consider the actual battleground. Is it located in 'favorable' or 'unfavorable ground,' or is the battleground virtually facilitated by conference audio or video calling technology?

The type of battle ground will ultimately inform your attack strategy and areas of flanking strategy.

Whatever type of battlefield it may be, you must seek to find the areas that give the most appropriate cover, and an escape route must always be established.

In guerrilla warfare, favorable ground is obviously preferred by the guerrilla and is usually inaccessible rural terrain, where the guerrilla can be most effective.

The larger regular army infantry, in view of their heavier artillery and equipment, must resort to using roads and established trails in order to move their arsenal effectively. This is where they become vulnerable, because convoys are always a preferred target for guerrillas.

Guerrillas are also, however, forced to fight in urban environments, termed 'unfavourable ground,' and cover and escape in these areas are not as abundant, so the guerrilla must rely on blending in with the local population in order to survive.

In the corporate world this is no different, employees are sometimes forced onto the roads in order to present work, essentially making them vulnerable to attack, so you must preplan all your movements and establish where you could be attacked by other guerrillas.

Throughout this book, the focus is on you as the protagonist guerrilla in order to guide you in your personal struggle in times of conflict, but you must understand that you are not the only guerrilla in the workplace and that all the other opponents that you have are fighting a guerrilla war against one another and also against you. It is not always irregular versus regular combat, because the majority of conflicts take place between guerrilla versus guerrilla.

You must also realize that you are a one man/woman band and will sometimes come up against a battalion of both regular and irregular opponents, so you must be aware of your limitations in this regard and be ready to preempt and respond to these attacks.

Ambushes by their very nature, we have learned, rely on the element of surprise. Therefore, to effectively counter them you must remove the element of surprise. Your movements within the corporate battlefield must be strategic and never sporadic; see it more like a game of chess and less like a game of dodgeball.

## Reconnaissance, Infiltration, and Espionage

In order to effectively preplan your movements, you must engage in reconnaissance and espionage.

Reconnaissance is the more passive of the two, involving looking at terrain maps and satellite photos in an attempt to gain information to inform strategy, whereas espionage implies a more active role in understanding your opponent.

### • Infiltration and Espionage

To learn more about your enemy and their strategy of attack, you must seek to infiltrate them either directly or indirectly. Infiltration involves seeking out an enemy's weak points in order to reside among them undetected so that information of various kinds can be gained.

To do this directly in the corporate world requires the guise of active displays of ulterior motives, in which you exhibit interest in one area but are really concerned with obtaining information on another.

By having information on one aspect of an enemy's operation, you can best estimate the condition, progress, or urgency of another. You must be extremely cautious not to expose your true intentions in these interactions.

An example of this is would be a large presentation that you are due to give to the department next week and that you know may have negative repercussions on some teams more than on others without being certain of which or of its true impact on everyone.

To find this out you need to essentially test the water beforehand with each stakeholder very subtly without giving the game away. This can be done by asking questions that appear unrelated but are actually elaborate mechanisms to receive small pieces of information to best make your assumption. If you sense that one team is due to be impacted more than others, you can then seek to arm yourself with the appropriate tailored response to this opponent when you have the public presentation so you will not be left exposed when they target you.

You must also be aware that guerrillas rely on the local population as effective cover because many can be aligned to their cause. So, bearing this in mind, you must be aware that your presence may be viewed as hostile.

Indirect infiltration involves using a third party to relay this information to you. This third party may or may not be aligned to you but can nevertheless be used to great advantage. Forewarned is indeed forearmed.

- **Reconnaissance**

Reconnaissance of your opponent will serve as significant armor in any incoming attack because you are armed with the appropriate information necessary to make the best response in times of conflict.

Corporate reconnaissance involves the utilization of key information related to your opponents. This can be as obtuse as spend analytics, staff turnover rates, budgetary variances, and any other information on your opponent that will identify patterns in their behavior. Other examples include seeking information on the details of historic decisions made by your opponent in order to find some precedent that may be related to your initiative or cause to repel any potential attacks. Your key objective in a battle is to seek to stop your opponent in their tracks during their potential onslaught by revealing to them (and the audience) information specific to them that portrays them as hypocritical.

Reconnaissance also looks at the terrain that you will be engaging in. Let's use the foregoing example again of a public presentation to a department. Your terrain will be the physical location of the presentation. Who will be there? Will it be virtual or over the telephone? In my experience of corporate conflict, I've found that people are less likely to attack when a meeting is in person as opposed to over the phone; this feeds into the near versus far ambush tactic but always has its exceptions.

You must seek to ascertain what senior management will be present because opponents will seek to use the senior management presence as leverage in their attack.

You must not rely solely on the interpretation of your stakeholder's personality profile to predict the direction of any potential conflict related to the consequences or fallout from the news that you are about to reveal in your presentation as many enemies may not have even revealed themselves yet.

Enemies and can take on many forms and the hidden enemy is always the most dangerous.

You must seek to obtain any information possible that will help you in countering any potential attack. You must operate as though an attack is inevitable, remembering Murphy's Law: "If it can happen, it will happen."

- **Tracking**

Tracking your opponent from a safe distance will also have its benefits. You must remember not to get too close and reveal yourself. You are essentially looking for patterns of behavior and times of each key interaction. Who are the allies of your opponent? What is their self-interest? The process of game theory feeds into this concept very well in seeking to find answers to these questions.

- **Scouting and Patrolling**

Scouting and patrolling are defensive actions that you carry out to help protect and reinforce your position. In the corporate world, conversely, this is carried out by testing the receptiveness of your opponent and benchmarking this against the resilience of your defenses. This is done by releasing small amounts of information about an upcoming change or via disinformation to gauge your opponent's self-interest levels.

# Ambush Strategy

Having evaluated the available reconnaissance and espionage information, you must now use it to inform what attack strategy your opponent may deploy against you. Ambush has always been the preferred attack strategy by guerrillas because it relies on the element of surprise and gives a smaller unit an advantage over a larger infantry but also against other guerrillas.

Ambushes can be categorized into the following three different types:

- **Deliberate Ambush**

  This is a preplanned attack on a target in which all prior information at your disposal has been evaluated and considered. This is the most effective form of ambush because your opponents have as much information on you as they can get before engaging you.

  In the corporate world, this is when your opponent has attempted to seek as much information on you as possible to use against you in a conflict situation. You must therefore always be careful not to reveal too much about yourself and your motivations because any information, even if minor, can be used against you in times of battle. This is not to say that you must remain a closed book but that you just need to be aware that your words and actions, however innocent or innocuous certain behavior may seem to you, may be of interest to someone who is always watching and taking notes.

  Your opponent will then use this information against you at a strategic point in time or place that they perceive will give them the most advantageous outcome. They could even lie in wait for months or even years for this opportunity to arise, so you must never discount an opponent's motivations over time.

- **Opportunity Ambush**

  Opportunity ambushes, as their namesake implies, are just that. They are situations in which you have been located by your opponents, and they essentially attack you in an opportunistic fashion.

  In the corporate world, opportunity ambushes arise in two situations. The first is that your opponent has done their homework on you and received relevant information on you in order to launch an effective attack but cannot find the correct battleground or outlet for the assault, so they become impatient and attack in a spontaneous fashion.

The second is that opportunity ambushes arise when an opponent has zero or partial information on you and chooses to attack without the appropriate planning.

- **Indirect Ambushes Using Secondary Forces**

  Technically a form of deception and characterized as a deliberate ambush, this method essentially relies on the enemy distracting you during battle and then seeking to catch you off guard by approaching from your rear in a secondary attack.

  A report was developed in 2012 by the International Association of Chiefs of Police (IACP) in the United States, as part of an initiative with CNA, the Department of Justice Office of Community Oriented Policing Services (COPS), and the IACP, to discuss and raise awareness on the subject of ambush assaults against law enforcement. Its statistics revealed some interesting insights in ambush strategies and defenses.

  Between 1990 and 2012 ambush classification revealed that 68 percent of all ambushes were spontaneous (opportunity) and 32 percent were entrapment (deliberate).

  The survival rates revealed that 41 percent of officers survived the entrapment ambush (deliberate) and 49 percent of officers survived the spontaneous ambush (opportunity).

## Summary

What this tells us is that spontaneous (opportunity) ambushes are the most utilized form of ambush but have the highest survival rate.

## Ambush Tactics

Once the potential ambush strategies of your opponents have been evaluated, you must now try and predict their tactics and respond as appropriately as possible. Referring back to our study of game theory, you may already have spotted patterns in your opponents' strategies and tactics, so you must now look at your own counterinsurgency techniques.

The following is a list of tactics used to carry out ambush strategies.

First, you must understand that ambushes fall into two distinctive categories but contain many subcategory permutations.

The two categories of ambush are as follows:

- **Near Ambush**

  A near ambush is usually characterized as taking place within 100 meters of your location, usually with your opponent using small arms fire. This can be advantageous for the attacker in view of the increased accuracy deriving from proximity but can also be negative because they are essentially within your grasp of retaliation, presenting risks for both parties.

- **Far Ambush**

  A far ambush is one that takes place beyond 100 meters of your location and outside the range of your effective retaliation. Snipers fall into this category because they are extremely hard to locate and effectively return fire on.

  This is an extremely difficult ambush to defend against because of the concealment of the attacker strategically located outside of your view and ultimate reach.

  When looking to counter ambushes you must remember that careful preplanning on your part is the best defense against these attacks because to be exposed to these types of attacks can sometimes mean that you have failed to prepare yourself appropriately.

The subcategories of both near and far ambushes are as follows:

- **Point Ambush**

  This is where your opponent freely enters a single location where they can be attacked. This position is known, informally, as the 'kill zone.'

  This tactic is preferred by your opponents because you are essentially positioned in an area that can be easily fired upon. You are effectively pushed into a corner; whether this is designed to force you to exhibit an attack response or, alternatively, as a process of annihilation, it goes without saying, that it is a dangerous position to find yourself in. Point ambushes can give rise to more deliberate ambushes because they are strategic in nature with the location setup and encounter preplanned by your opponent.

- **Area Ambush**

  An area ambush is essentially where there is more than one kill zone and essentially features multiple point ambush locations. This can be a much more difficult tactic for your opponent to carry off because the battle will be spread out over a larger area rather than contained as in a single point ambush. It can also be the result of multiple attempts to corner you in a series of engagements. You have a better chance of surviving this type of ambush because you have more maneuverability. These types of ambushes generally result in opportunity ambushes owing to the unpredictability of the environment and the difficulty of being able to see where or when an opponent will attack.

- **I-Shaped Ambush**

  This is the most basic ambush tactic in that one side fires on the other from opposite sides of the target's linear path of movement.

  In the corporate world this ambush tactic is utilized to keep you moving between two points and is designed to encourage you not to stop. This is when opponents want you out of their area and do not want you to focus on something they wish to keep hidden or protected.

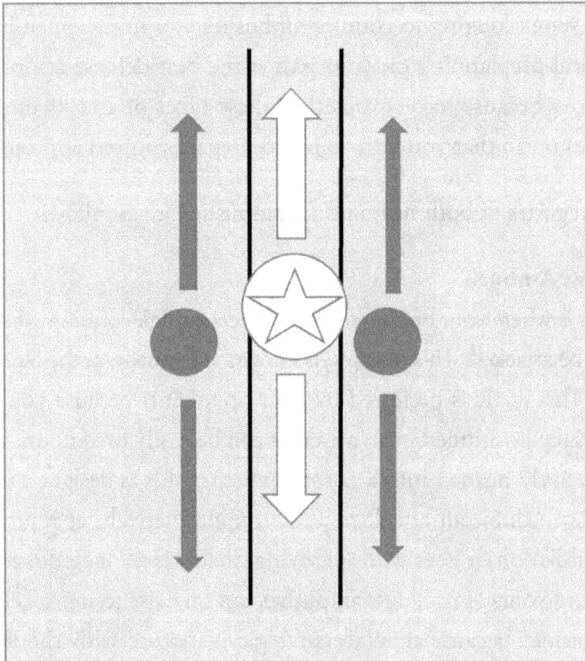

*Figure 5.1* I-shaped ambush

**Effective Counterinsurgency Methods**

You must go with the flow in encounters like this and move out of the kill zone as you are being directed. They do not care which way you flee as long as it takes you away from their area. You have essentially uncovered something that is being overzealously guarded. It has now piqued your interest, however, and your opponents have effectively shown their hands, so you can now attempt to revisit this position via stealth.

You must also highlight to your opponent and all present that you are moving on while subtly inferring to everyone that they have something to hide.

• **T-shaped Ambush**
A T-shaped ambush is where an opponent is attacked from a perpendicular angle with restriction, inhibited on both sides by rough terrain. The only escape in this tactic is retreat or withdrawal.

The corporate equivalent of this tactic is when an opponent is defending their position against your advance with the sole intention of pushing you backward and discouraging your progression.

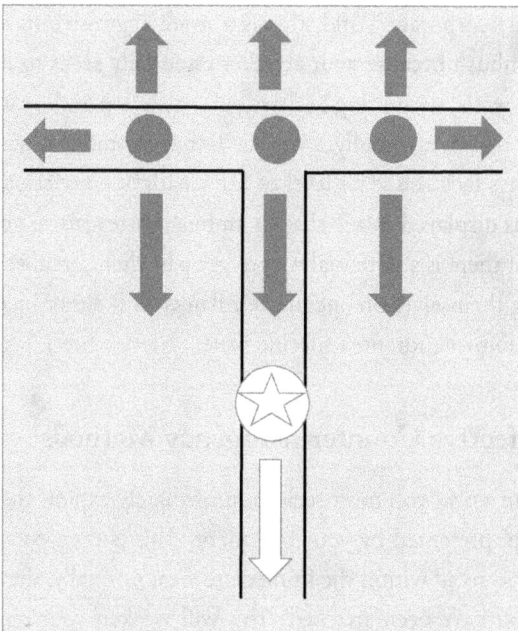

*Figure 5.2* T-shaped ambush

### Effective Counterinsurgency Methods

In this scenario, the attackers are defending a static position and are forcing you to retreat in one direction, thereby effectively forcing you to back down in your course of action. They have chosen this environment that is effectively designed to push you in one direction, which is exactly the opposite direction from which you came.

This rough terrain is essentially using unorthodox techniques obtained from information that you have secured as part of your reconnaissance activities. You will pull information seemingly from left field and will surprise and disorient your opponent.

To effectively counter this ambush, you must be prepared to face the onslaught that your opponent brings to the situation, and you can do this only by being forearmed with the relevant knowledge and facts mentioned previously.

- **L-shaped Ambush**

An L-shaped ambush occurs when an attack is launched from two positions. The long linear part of the L provides parallel firing directed at your position, and the short leg of the L is where fire will come from a head-on or rear position that will limit your escape in that direction.

In the corporate world, this is a more aggressive form of the linear ambush because your attacker essentially seeks to halt your progress while attempting to drive you backward at the same time.

This is also, essentially, a weaker T-shaped ambush, where your opponent's lack the same level of information, conviction, or discipline as displayed in a T-shaped ambush. It reveals to you, however, that there is a potential way to get past them because they are exposing themselves on one of their flanks with either incorrect or missing information on a specific issue.

## Effective Counterinsurgency Methods

In the corporate world you must seek to immediately exploit the erroneous information presented by your opponent. This is then conveyed by you in a response to all within the immediate area, normally, the meeting room where you have been attacked. This will weaken your opponent's resolve and ensure safe passage.

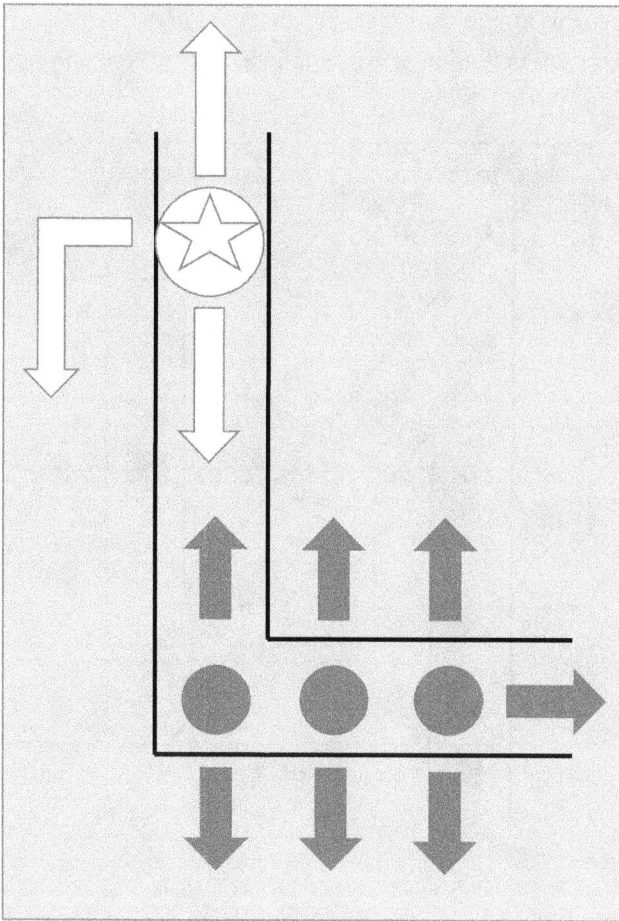

**Figure 5.3** *L-shaped ambush*

- **N/Z-shaped Ambush**

   An "N" or "Z"-shaped corporate ambush is, essentially, a more robust L-shaped ambush, the only difference being that an additional smaller leg is now present that attacks you from the rear. It does not, however, completely immobilize you, but you may have to abandon your position and attempt to go off road to survive this attack. Again, this rough terrain, essentially, uses unorthodox techniques obtained from information that you have secured as part of your reconnaissance activities. You will pull information again seemingly from left field and will surprise and disorient your opponent.

This formation is more psychological in nature because it tries to create an illusion of claustrophobia to force you off track.

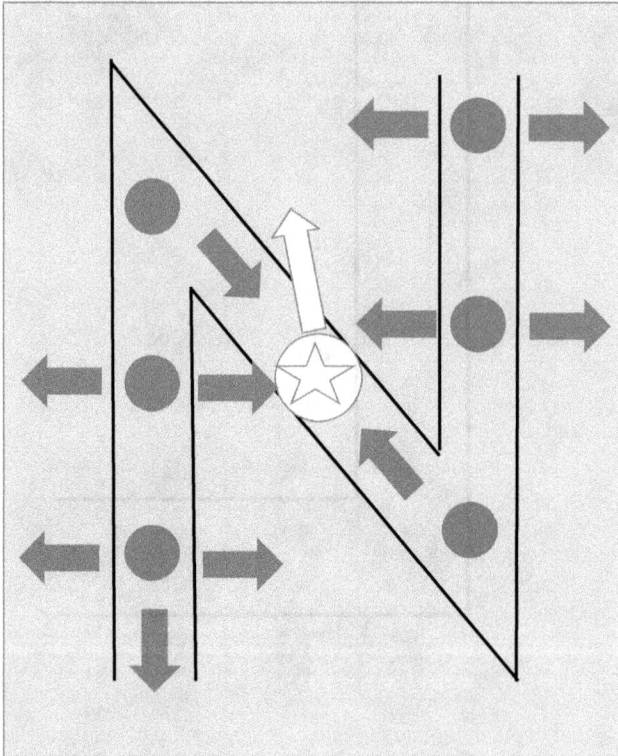

**Figure 5.4** *N/Z-shaped ambush*

### Effective Counterinsurgency Methods

Corporate "N" ambushes are those in which your opponent seeks to box you in from opposing angles but have not secured the rough terrain that you can seek refuge in during this attack. As in other ambush formation defenses, this rough terrain, essentially, uses unorthodox techniques obtained from information that you have secured as part of your reconnaissance activities. You will again pull information from left field and will surprise and disorient your opponent.

- **V-shaped Ambush**
  A V-shaped ambush is one in which an attack is launched from two linear positions deployed alongside your movements that

culminates in a point. This increases the firepower concentrated in your direction.

If you find yourself in this position, you are essentially cornered. This is one of the hardest positions to defend because your only chance of survival is to advance through the fire, and your opponent is acutely aware of this fact. It is designed to make you fight them and baits you into battle.

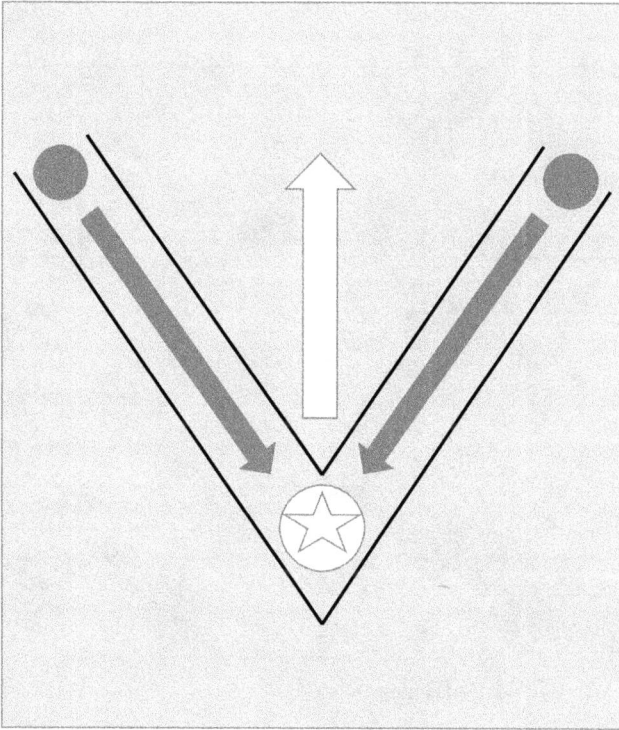

*Figure 5.5* V-shaped ambush

### Effective Counterinsurgency Methods

In this position there in no option but to return fire, this firepower being the information and facts that you have from your reconnaissance activities and is your only source of weaponry and ammunition. Without this you are essentially defeated. You must be aware of any V-shaped point battles in your day-to-day activities and only seek to enter them when you are confident of your strengths in relation to your opponent's.

- **C/U-Shaped Ambush**

  A "C" or "U"-shaped ambush is, essentially, another modification to the standard L-shaped ambush tactic, whereby another longer leg is added to the position to form an approximate semicircle around you, increasing your opponent's firepower and surrounding you. This tactic is usually the result of a botched V-shaped ambush because you have more wiggle room and are not so narrowly cornered.

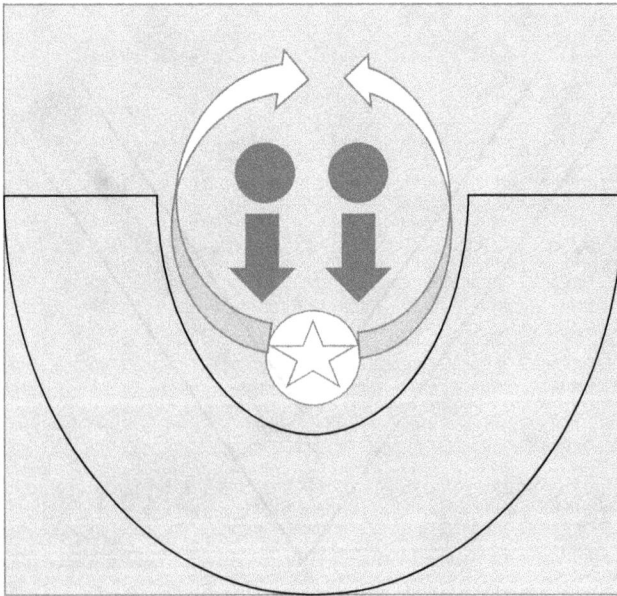

*Figure 5.6* C/U-shaped ambush

### Effective Counterinsurgency Methods

This will have similar attributes to a V-shaped ambush but without the point cornering aspect. You have been corralled but not completely cornered, so there is a better chance of escape. What this means is that your opponent, while having the relevant information on you, has failed to execute the delivery of their strategy effectively, making for a lesser impact than envisaged. Although you are wounded, you are not defeated yet and must seek to take cover, capitalizing on this failed attempt while returning fire.

## Positions with Increased Level of Difficulties

- **X-Shaped Ambush**

  This is, essentially, four interlocking V positions forcing you into one position in the center. Escape here is next to impossible, so you are forced to battle.

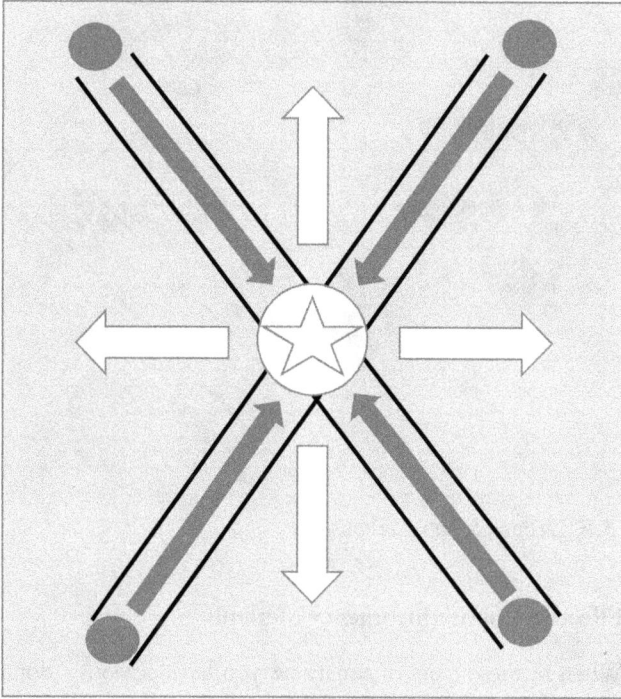

**Figure 5.7** *X-shaped ambush*

### Effective Counterinsurgency Methods

To effectively get out of this position you must return fire on the basis of a priority or ranking system. A rapid assessment of each attack must be calculated and prioritized; start with the most manageable attack and work your way up until all other attacks are addressed effectively.

- **Diamond Formation**

  This is, essentially, a permutation of the V-shaped tactic discussed earlier, with the opponent surrounded on all sides, and is, essentially, interlocking V-shaped positions that box the enemy in on all sides.

You have no option of escape and your only recourse is to push the nuclear button, taking yourself out in the process.

**Figure 5.8** *Diamond-shaped ambush*

### Effective Counterinsurgency Methods

When in these types of situations, you have obviously done something significant to incur the wrath of multiple people; maybe you have exposed something or uncovered malpractice where the threat to all involved is so severe that they seek to collectively threaten you. Surrender is less likely than that of a 'V' formation because of the number of opponents involved and the knowledge obtained, so your best chance of survival here is by defecting to their side (not recommended) or pushing the nuclear button. The nuclear button in this case can take many forms but is usually the one thing that you didn't imagine you would ever have to do, whatever it is.

- **Other Defensive Tactics**

Other counterinsurgency techniques can be more passive than others. An example of this derives from the animal kingdom, where prey attempts to starve out predators and is known as 'predator satiation.' This also happens in warfare as a passive war of attrition, where a standoff can take weeks and normally results in one side losing interest and moving on.

This can also be adopted in the corporate world and is carried out when you, essentially, do not give your opponent an opportunity to attack you. This is done not by fleeing or concealment but simply by being on the 'A-game' at all times. Your opponent will seek to find opportunities to attack and use information against you, so you must seek to limit the information provided or limit their ability to use it effectively, or indeed at all.

Let's revisit the IACP statistics:

The report summarizes the survival rates of officers against various dynamic characteristics on how the officer reacts to the ambush:

When officers wore body armor, they were 53 percent more likely to survive an attack compared with 30 percent if they did not wear body armor. Officers who took cover also had a 68 percent survival rate, compared with 39 percent if they did not take cover, and officers who returned fire were 68 percent more likely to survive an attack compared with 30 percent for those who did not return fire.

## Summary

What this tells us is that an officer who has the protective armor, seeks cover and returns fire stands a higher chance of surviving an ambush than one who does not do all three. So a dominant strategy on combination can be employed.

This also highlights the benefits of returning fire when under attack.

## Skirmishes

In all conflict situations, the differences between a skirmish and other methods of attack must be understood. Skirmishes happen in every conflict and are characterized by short, usually less powerful battles that can be a precursor to a much larger battle, with the skirmishers acting in a vanguard capacity to its larger battalion. Skirmishes can therefore be tactical and deceptive.

Expending all your ammunition and energy on a skirmish is therefore counterproductive because you will be exposed to the larger enemy waiting in the wings.

Corporate skirmishes involve baiting or harassment that is aimed at you by a small group of individuals or even by a single person. This is basically done to provoke you or lead you somewhere with the ultimate aim of setting you up for an attack that is yet to materialize.

You must therefore learn to differentiate between skirmishes and an offensive regular battle. Skirmishes can be characterized by an unusually high level of restraint exhibited by the attacking battalion and also by observing and identifying delay tactics such as patterns of fire varying between short rapid bursts and prolonged single shots.

Despite these observations, however, one can really discern the difference only over time as patterns can be observed in your opponents, so you will normally utilize a few strategic retreats before you are fully wise to these tricks.

## Other Offensive Tactics Utilized by Opponents

Apart from the 'lie in wait,' 'surprise and conquer' ambush styles detailed earlier, there are other methods of guerrilla warfare that are also used by your opponents.

- **Corporate Sabotage**
  Corporate sabotage is when your opponent seeks to derail your progress by indirect means rather than via ambushes. This is carried out by seeking to destroy various successful behaviors or actions that will contribute to your overall success or progress within a specific initiative. The main method of sabotage in the corporate world is carried out via booby traps.

- **Booby Traps**
  The use of booby traps in conflict greatly assists the combatants because not only is it a physical assistance during combat, but it also has psychological associations as combatants will naturally be suspicious of certain terrains owing to the potential presence of these devices.

### Effective Counterinsurgency Methods

The only way to effectively counter the presence of booby traps is to remove their psychological threat or hold that they have on you. This is done by assuming that they are everywhere, and you do this by holding a healthy suspicion of unfamiliar behavior and actions displayed by opponents.

- **Corporate Terrorism**

  Corporate terrorism is designed to instill fear into the recipient and is usually carried out to deter behavior or movements that seek to implement or enforce policies that do not take into consideration their repercussions or impacts experienced by a certain group as a result of these policies.

  Corporate terrorism is characterized by attacks perpetrated against you by your enemy who does not care about the impact that these attacks will have on others around you. Corporate terrorism always inflicts casualties on the innocent and uninvolved and can also be carried out when your enemies are unable to isolate you from your defended base and place of strength, so the entire base is targeted.

  So, essentially, if an opponent wishes to attack you, they can also see those close to you as targets.

  Corporate terrorism will have drastic negative effects on the brand or image of the perpetrator, but sometimes this is the point of the operation: to be respected through fear.

  Terrorism can also be described as a desperate act of an opponent to gain recognition or attention and will normally turn the general population against the terrorist so there will always be pressure from others to seek the best possible solution.

### Effective Counterinsurgency Methods

The only way to stop corporate terrorism is through effective politics by those in positions of power or significant influence.

Open battle against terrorists is not always recommended or even possible because of the hidden nature of the perpetrators. Successful counterterrorism methods take the form of dialogue with a negotiated peace with concessions made and given by both sides. You are effectively encouraging your attacker to use political peaceful means in an attempt to achieve their goals in these circumstances.

Sometimes, however, giving a political voice or even recognizing terrorism gives it an indirect credibility, so you must be very careful in taking any actions that validate their cause to the wider public, essentially giving them strength. Corporate terrorism is always carried out by your opponents who seek to gain leverage in certain negotiations so their motivations must always be exposed either to them, on a personal level, or publicly, to the wider population.

Only you must choose whether to eradicate the threat outright or negotiate with the threat because all instances are different and there is no single golden solution.

You must always seek to protect the vulnerable and innocent from being further harmed regardless of the course of action that you choose.

Repeated displays of corporate terrorism against you highlights, however, that you (and/or the wider organization) have failed to deal with the problem effectively, so this must inform the next move.

## Collateral Damage

Collateral damage is the accidental or unintended level of casualties resulting from your operations and activities. All statistics on possible collateral damage should be evaluated before engaging your opponent. The fallout and repercussions to uninvolved personnel should always have the goal of zero in any attack consideration, so you must be cognizant of the ripples and effects that your actions will have on the wider population. This should form the basis of your overall strategy.

## Summary

There are three parties to every war: "one side," "the other side," and the innocent population caught up in the middle. Each combatant will have their own definition of sabotage, terrorism, and collateral damage, although these definitions do not matter to the innocent population.

## False Flags

False flag attacks, although technically a form of deception, are attacks of sabotage or terrorism against you or others carried out by an opponent who makes it appear that it was someone else who perpetrated the attack.

Conversely, it can happen that an opponent can carry out an attack against someone else but blame you.

## Effective Counterinsurgency Methods

The only way to combat false flag operations is by having recourse to effective intelligence. Retaliation must also be preserved until you are in full possession of all the facts. This is why all fire must be held to avoid attacking the wrong opponent. A study of your perceived opponents' motivations may also draw you to an incorrect conclusion as to who is actually responsible for the attack, so you must seek to understand all the beneficiaries and stakeholders involved in any given prized action or decision.

All the foregoing scenarios and examples highlight the kinds of strategies your opponent can use to attack you and the best type of response. Sometimes, however, attack is the best form of defense, so the following active strategies can be utilized to best defeat your opponents.

## Offensive Strategies and Tactics Used by You against Your Opponents

- **Driving**

  Driving is the process of moving or directing your opponent to a position where you need them to be in order to gain a battle advantage. This can be done passively via booby trapping certain areas that they will instinctively avoid or avoid only after they have incurred a casualty. By indirectly highlighting to your opponent the areas where they cannot go, they are therefore corralled into taking a route that they would not normally take, a route that will leave them exposed to attack.

  Another method of driving is the more active method of shooting in their direction in an attempt to move them into positions that they are more exposed to. Similar to the earlier example of the U.S. armies in Iraq and Afghanistan, this method will usually involve a lot of ammunition and so should be attempted only if enough ammunition reserves are available.

Corporate driving takes place when you have full visibility of your enemies' motivation or payload and look to exploit those facts by pushing them in a direction that makes them more vulnerable to attack.

- **Flushing**
Flushing is a technique whereby you are aware of a potential enemy location but use other sources to flush them out of their position and into an awaiting attack.

In hunting animals, these other sources are usually dogs, which scare the prey into fleeing their location.

The corporate equivalent of flushing is to use a shared opponent to assist in your operation. The actions of the shared opponent can be either active or passive, conscious or subconscious, but no matter what their motivation, it is you who have actively sought to make it happen.

This can be in the form of a senior manager or stakeholder that will be affected in some way or from an opponent's strategy that has been revealed to you by effective information. By flushing the enemy out of hiding, they are effective exposed and therefore easily beaten.

- **Spotlighting**
Spotlighting is a method of hunting whereby the attackers search for their animal prey at nightfall making use of reflective eye shine, using large spotlights either on foot or mounted on an off-road vehicle. The animals do not instinctively recognize the light source as being a danger, so they curiously remain still or approach the source to better understand it and in so doing are trapped or killed.

The corporate equivalent is, essentially, psychological entrapment and is carried out by revealing information that renders your opponent curious and wanting more details on an issue that appeals to their self-serving nature. They therefore refuse to back away or are drawn to you and toward the answers. You have, essentially, blinded them and diverted their focus onto one situation only, (as in the flypaper theory) and other issues on the periphery that can be more critical can now be carried out away from their watchful gaze.

## Strategies for Dealing with Difficult People

When seeking to understand or predict the various psychological motivations exhibited by your opponent to best deal with perceived or apparent attacks, you must understand that people within the workplace normally fall into two camps: They are either 'rational' or 'irrational' in their thoughts and actions.

A lot of the foregoing techniques can be more appealing when dealing with opponents who are deemed rational because it results in them behaving or acting in certain ways that can be predicted.

It will show that they are likely to amicably accept defeat or push a certain agenda based on a shared reference of the information present in any given situation.

But what happens if you are dealing with an irrational opponent whose behavior cannot be so easily predicted? You must therefore seek to find patterns in displays of irrational behavior to best predict your opponent's response.

Let's look at the type of psychological factors that lead to this irrationality in corporate animals.

They are driven mainly by innate biological emotions.

## Human Emotions

In the late 20th century, psychologist Paul Ekman theorized that there were six human emotions:

***Happiness, Sadness, Fear, Disgust, Anger, and Surprise***

A recent study, published in the *Proceedings of National Academy of Sciences*, however, revealed that there were indeed 27 types of human emotions:

*Admiration, Adoration, Aesthetic Appreciation, Amusement, Anxiety, Awe, Awkwardness, Boredom, Calmness, Disgust, Empathetic pain,*

*Entrancement, Envy, Excitement, Fear, Horror, Interest, Joy, Nostalgia,*
*Sadness, Satisfaction, Sexual desire, Sympathy, and Triumph*

If we seek to best understand the emotions displayed by our opponents, we can use this information to inform our strategies and tactics in
all interactions with our opponents.

Let's look at the most commonly displayed emotions that cause conflict within the corporate office.

### Anxiety, Fear

Anxiety arises out of uneasiness and fear of the unknown. Human beings
are naturally fearful in times of change or uncertainty, and sometimes
having a healthy fear keeps us on our guard, but when a fear starts to
overcome us and begins to affect our decision making or actions, it's time
to make changes to keep it in balance.

A fearful or anxious person can be dangerous in that they will act to
protect their survival without knowing the full information, and this can
lead to conflict within workplaces. Animals in the wild that sense fear always attack because they view this fear as a threat as they do not fully trust
your intentions; the same also applies in the corporate world. Opponents
can attack you if they sense an anxiety within you because they see this as
a vulnerability in you that could threaten their own performance.

Fear and anxiety can also be detrimental to an entire department as
the fear can spread like the 'domino theory' perceived in the cold war era.
The only way to relieve fear is by giving effective communication.

You must be careful, however, not to reduce all fear in an opponent
because, as discussed earlier, a small amount of fear is healthy and can
keep our interaction in check. If you completely seek to remove the fear
from your opponent, you will also be seen as vulnerable. One key lesson
to learn is that you should never downplay your natural behavior or abilities to make someone else feel better about themselves.

When dealing with anxious and fearful people, you must seek resolutions in every interaction. These are not insincere resolutions, however, but
actual resolutions that will lead to a decreased amount of fear on their part
if it is your actions that will cause them or their department any hardship.

This is carried out via effective communication, whereby you summarize the issue, display empathy with their insecurities, and end every conversation with: "I'm glad we've reached agreement here" or "I'm glad we found a way forward." This highlights to them that you are open to their plight and that a window of opportunity is open to them in order to give their input on a situation that affects them in the pursuit of your objectives.

### Disgust, Awkwardness

Disgust is an obvious strong reaction to a decision or action that is taken or being considered.

Awkwardness implies a mild and sometimes subtle and uncomfortable reaction to a scenario or initiative.

People who display feelings of disgust or awkwardness overtly are useful as they are a natural instinctive litmus test benchmark to any endeavor you wish to undertake or have taken.

These feelings must not be ignored, and feedback must be sought from the relevant people as to why they feel put off by this course of action.

### Envy

This emotion cuts across our own psychological insecurities and highlights our competitive tendencies.

You must be mindful of the differences between envy and jealousy. While both interrelated, envy is an emotion displayed by someone when they lack an attribute that someone else possesses that they deem desirable. Jealousy is the fear associated with a person being threatened that a possession that they already have may be taken away from them.

You must therefore seek to understand whether your opponents are either jealous or envious of you before you can best design your strategy to deal with them.

Let's first look at the envious opponent in the workplace. You may have something that they don't have, perhaps a position of seniority, a qualification, expertise level, or even a skill, and usually they do not have it or cannot obtain it. This fact therefore makes them feel threatened by you and their behavior toward you will reflect that. They will usually be cold and distant or, if in your vicinity, may shower you with false praise or even refuse to recognize any achievements or downplay them if they actually do. You will pick up on the insincerity of this false praise normally, but if not, it will usually leave you feeling that something is just not right and that you can't put your finger on it. This is usually how envy manifests itself.

Jealous opponents are threatened in an entirely different manner; they see you as being a threat to something that they have; this is normally a status that they hold within the department as being a subject matter expert that they fear you could take the glory away from them.

As in dealing with anxious and fearful opponents, you should never downplay your natural behavior or abilities to make someone else feel better about themselves or less threatened by you.

You must ask yourself, why does it bother me that this person or group of people are envious or jealous of me? Do you possess such a lack of self-confidence and assurance that you require everyone to like you? Do you require their validation? If the answer is yes to any of these questions, it indicates that your ego is out of balance and must be readjusted.

You will learn in time that having envious and jealous opponents is not only a good thing, but also a yardstick of success.

### Anger, Sadness

Anger is an unsubtle psychological response that reveals our true feelings on a matter.

Sadness is also a psychological response that reveals our true feelings on a matter but can often be concealed. I have grouped these two emotions together because they are closely interlinked. Anger is, essentially, a form of repressed sadness.

Once overt displays of anger are displayed in the office, it's game over; the opponent has given away their true feelings and position and is now vulnerable to present and future attacks, so no matter how angry you feel in the corporate world, you must never truly reveal this to your opponent(s).

To control someone who is displaying anger toward you or another person, the following guidelines are important:

1. You must never return fire by shouting back, because this will only raise the emotional level and intensity of the exchange; you must deliver your responses in a calm and controlled manner.

2. Draw awareness to their mood; inform the person that their behavior is unacceptable. (This may seem illogical but does work, especially if others are present.)

3. You must try and keep the focus of the situation in the present and not the past. The angry person will always try and drag you back to situations of past indiscretions, so always try and bring the issue back to the present.

4. You must highlight to the angry person that you are listening to them and taking on board what they have to say. You do this effectively by relating back to them points that they have said in summary form to show that you are listening.

5. You must seek to empathize with the angry person. Empathy, however, does not mean compromising. It merely shows to them that you understand why they feel this way.

6. Be aware of your body language and facial expression. If an angry person realizes that they are not affecting you with their loud and aggressive behavior, they will resist quicker because they will realize that they are the one who is overreacting, especially if it's in public.

7. When things calm down and after some time has passed, this is when you confront the angry person again, reminding them of the unacceptability of their behavior.

8. Learn to recognize signs of when these tactics are not working, and remove yourself from the situation.

All of this can be easier said than done when a person is screaming at you. Only over time will you learn to adopt these principles effectively, because anger when directed at us sometimes brings out our own primal response mechanisms. You must know your audience and your environment, however, and not cause yourself or your brand any unnecessary damage.

One point to note in these situations is that you do not always have to have a resolution to the problem at hand, because sometimes just listening and conveying empathy to the upset person is more than enough to lighten their load. The same principles apply to instances where you are angry or sad, and sometimes just sharing the problem with someone is more than enough to lighten the burden and help with your maneuverability when back in the jungle environment.

The above four groups of corporate emotions can often lead to other negative scenarios if allowed to get out of balance:

These include the following:

## Rivalries and Vendettas

Owing to the intense emotions and behavior in such a small space, rivalries and vendettas are always present in corporate jungles. As discussed earlier, the utopian scenario is to have no enemies, or as close to zero as possible, because the baggage associated with having enemies usually clouds your judgment and adversely affects your overall maneuverability and effectiveness. The reality, however, is that having enemies can be outside of your control because you may not extol the same label of enemy that is extolled to you. It must also be understood that having enemies can also be an indication of your success or progress and that, therefore, enemies are sometimes a necessary evil.

> *So you have enemies? Good! That means you've stood up for something,*
> *sometime in your life*
> —Modernization of Victor Hugo quote from "Villemain"

You must also learn to distinguish between the definitions of opponent and enemies, as discussed in Chapter 2; this distinction will assist you in choosing your strategy in relation to a specific rivalry. You must learn that rivalries are normally impersonal in nature as part of the natural competition of survival, but when a rivalry becomes personal it becomes a vendetta.

A vendetta implies a personal or emotional stake in a conflict.

You must therefore seek to limit your rivalries from becoming vendettas wherever possible. This, however, is easier said than done, but in order to ensure your survival you must adapt to learning when to fight and when not to fight.

# Bullying

This is a topic that always needs to be discussed.

Bullying is undoubtedly a cancer in any organization, but you will be surprised to find that some organizations actually misinterpret or play down its occurrence as part of their own specific policies and culture aimed at promoting intense competition and worker is turned against worker in a quest to get the prize.

A recent study by online recruitment firm *monster.com* revealed that over 90 percent of the survey respondents of over 200 people had admitted to experiencing bullying in the workplace. Over half of those surveyed (51 percent) claimed that this was at the hands of a manager, and 39 percent claimed they were bullied by a coworker or coworkers.

Bullying is the worst experience that anyone can feel at work, and you must learn not only to defeat it, but also to recognize its traits. You must also be aware of yourself being a bully or exhibiting bullying behavior toward others. Bullying is a scourge and must be stamped out of all organizations, and you should never, under any circumstances, put up with it.

# Identifying and Dealing with a Bully

To effectively deal with a bully, you must first identify them. This may sound unusual, but people commonly do not realize that they are being bullied. Bullying can be swift and apparent from your first initial encounter of interactions with a person, but it can also be incremental, starting slowly and working its way up over time, leading to you dealing with it subconsciously by saying to yourself, "Me, bullied? No, no way; that's just John; he's always like that." Well, that's no excuse for John's behavior, whoever he is.

Bullying will always make your stomach feel as if you have just been punched.

You will probably adopt many techniques to deal with this, such as the techniques we studied in Chapter 2, namely, suppression denial, anger, or divergence, but you must realize that the only effective way to deal with a bully is to confront them.

When confronting them you are taking the power back into your own hands. This is easier said than done, however, particularly when confronting a member of the organization who has been there decades or even your own manager for that matter. It really doesn't matter, however, as when you stand up to a bully you are standing up for your own integrity. Integrity differs from an imbalanced ego in that integrity encompasses your self-belief system and shows how you treat others and how you like to be treated in return. If you compromise your integrity you are compromising yourself as a human being.

It may be the most fearful thing that you ever do, but you must take the bully aside and tell them that their behavior is unacceptable. You do not ever have to give information on how it made you feel, because this is allowing yourself to be vulnerable in their presence. So simply telling them you will not stand for their behavior any longer is powerful and effective enough. A bully normally uses an advantage that they have over others as a cowardly way of appearing powerful to feed their own imbalanced ego and insecurities that they usually possess. This can be either a position of seniority or long tenure but you must understand that bullies normally have inferiority complexes and are easily beaten by strong and determined people with conviction. So you must never underestimate the ability that you have in overcoming and defeating a bully.

You must also realize that some bullies may have never been told this before and have moved through life with hardly any challenges, so they may take this encounter as an attack. Normally, however, a bully will more than likely have been made aware of this fact before, so all attempts to downplay the situation or appear shocked are merely an act.

Once you have confronted a bully, you have exposed them, in the same way a songbird signals to the predator that they have been discovered and for the predator to give up the hunt, which they ultimately do. You are essentially showing the bully that he or she has revealed themselves to you. Whether you are junior or senior does not matter, and you must always relay this information to the bully. It will not threaten your job, because a bully will never seek to tell anyone that they have been called a bully, so the situation will usually resolve itself via awkwardness at first, with the bully, eventually acting as though it didn't happen.

This is not always the case, however, as bullies will naturally slip into their old behavior, so you must constantly remind them if something is unacceptable or inappropriate to you.

You must also seek to establish whether even one bullying attempt is one too far.

This approach requires a certain type of brazenness from the outset in order to be effective, which can be achieved only through self-confidence. It will seem daunting, but you must have a level of self-respect that permeates every human interaction and must stand up for yourself when you feel that a line has been crossed regardless of the perpetrator at hand. I must stress, however, that any instances of racism and/or discrimination on gender, religious beliefs, and sexual preference must be considered red lines and must be reported.

## Benefits and Limitations of Engaging HR

In all dealings with a bully you must make someone else aware of the situation. This can be a trusted coworker partner, friend, or parent because this person will be necessary in keeping you focused on the resolution. You may at times opt to seek the assistance of Human Resources, but you must be aware of both the positives and the limitations that this can have.

I do not mean that HR professionals will be ineffective against bullying, but you must realize that some HR departments will seek to protect the company first and you a distant second.

If your bully is your manager, HR may fall down on the manager's side to protect the organization.

HR departments will smother you in policy, because they will also seek to protect themselves in any perceived case of bullying, given that they are ultimately responsible for their employee's mental health and well-being.

I have been involved with some HR departments that have buried their heads in the sand when faced with undeniable facts and documented evidence of bullying by senior managers, because they are afraid of unraveling the fabric of the corporate material that keeps them covered.

You should, for this very reason, always seek to resolve the situation yourself before engaging HR.

There are many HR departments, however, that deal with bullying extremely effectively, so you must never tar them all with the same brush. I merely raise this point to drive you toward a self-resolution before you go formal, because going formal isn't always the best method for reasons already mentioned.

HR can be viewed like any other department in an organization: You can have high-performing ones, and you can have poor performing ones.

An effective HR department will seek to resolve the issue and will first seek mediation between you and the bully. This is a very powerful form of dispute resolution, because it will result in both sides sitting down with a mediator to get to the bottom of any issue and to seek a way forward.

The question arises, however, whether you should have tried that yourself before engaging HR. It will show the bully that you have strength and conviction to take them on, with HR being used as a deterrent to the bully in order to find a resolution. This form of vigilantism is not advised by HR departments, but it is effective in situations where bullying is present.

## Defending Coworkers

This is always an emotive subject. Should you intervene when you see someone else being bullied?

In the wild, documentary makers never intervene when a jaguar catches an antelope; they let nature take its course. This, however, is painful and traumatic to watch, and I have always intervened when I have seen wrongdoing in the workplace, though sometimes to my detriment. Interventions, however, do not always have to be confrontations with the perpetrator; you can simply raise the subject with the victim or others in the vicinity, advising them that the events that you just witnessed were unacceptable. By simply highlighting and confirming the gravity of the situation, it can empower the victim to stand up for themselves. Sometimes victims will be in a state of denial or experiencing Stockholm syndrome, as we have seen in the previous chapter, so waking them up is all that is required.

# Hierarchies

When discussing your effectiveness in all interactions with your opponent and being able to counter any attacks, you must also be conscious of the hierarchy displayed in the corporate environment.

This hierarchy applies in the animal kingdom too, where many species have systems of order to ensure collective survival, such as an alpha status within the pack.

The corporate world differs, however, because these systems of hierarchy are essentially conscious forms of regulation to keep everyone at their station and avoid anarchy. This can also be said in military outfits where ranks are also present, but what happens if your attacker is actually of a higher rank than you, a rank that affords them all the necessary protection and cover and allows them to act almost with impunity toward anyone or everyone below them or in their path.

What if you are actually much stronger and fitter (more intelligent and more capable) than your manager but are not the official alpha of the pack?

This is where your manager engages in what I like to call 'self cannibalism,' that is, a manager being threatened by the strength or abilities of a subordinate (or multiple subordinates) in their own team and seeking to threaten the progression of this individual or individuals within their team, which therefore leads to their own ultimate demise.

Rivalries with your own management can have serious implications for your mental health and well-being.

The origins of rivalries with your manager must be understood if they are to be dealt with effectively.

An effective approach requires that you view your manager as you would any other individual in the workplace. They are, essentially, your opponents because there are always consequences to you for not fulfilling objectives, so managers can be categorized as a threat like all other threats.

As with all your opponents, this does suggest that you should express hostility, but the presence of healthy suspicion must be taken at all times to ensure your survival.

Conflict can arise within teams when an employee either disagrees with or undervalues the contribution expressed by their manager. In many cases this is not misplaced, however, because the manager could actually be weak or poor in regard to overall effectiveness. This realization by the subordinate(s) can result in a buildup of resentment toward the manager and can sometimes spill out into various actions and behaviors.

You must also be aware that your manager, although part of the same team, also views you as an opponent, because your strengths and weaknesses are constantly being evaluated to get a fix on your overall effectiveness, and having a subordinate that is either too strong or too weak will threaten the manager's survival.

Inept managers, in my experience, fall into two distinct groups: "Consciously inept" or "unconsciously inept."

### Unconsciously Inept Managers

In 1999, two scientists, David Dunning and Justin Kruger, hypothesized what is now referred to as the Dunning–Kruger effect. This is present when people with low ability overestimate their true level of ability in a given situation or series of situations. There can be many reasons for this, such as an imbalanced ego or narcissism but it is theorized that inept people do not know that they are inept owing to a lack of capacity or intelligence required to understand the actualities.

### Consciously Inept Managers

The other classification of inept manager is "consciously inept," or what I refer to as a 'conscious bluffer.' This is where a manager is aware of their own shortcomings, which they seek to keep hidden in an attempt to ensure their own survival. Diligent subordinates can often spot this behavior, which can lead to hostility.

To effectively deal with an inept manager, you will therefore need to distinguish between the two categories and base your strategy of dealing with them on the correct definition.

- **Dealing with an Unconsciously Inept Manager**
  Unconsciously inept managers, as discussed earlier, will not have any indication of their inabilities or ineffectiveness, so any attempts

to draw awareness or raise your concerns to them will more than likely seem like attacks to them. You must, therefore, be able to 'manage the manager' as your conscious awareness is therefore an advantage over their unconscious behaviors so you must seek to learn their limitations and look for patterns. These patterns can therefore serve as critical pieces of information that may be used either to distract or to deter your manager, resulting in you getting your tasks completed. One thing to remember, however, is never to feign praise to your manager for their behaviors, because you will only be facilitating or enabling their behavior, impeding your own future success. Your main tactics here in getting the tasks completed are distraction and diversion.

You must remember that the presence of an unconsciously inept manager does not automatically mean that the manager will possess misplaced loyalties or mistrust toward their team; it just means that they are unaware that they are incapable of completing the task at hand.

- **Dealing with a Consciously Inept Manager**
This is by far the worst type of manager to have, because every interaction that they engage in with you and their teams is carefully orchestrated and methodical so as to not to reveal their ineptness.

They will be overly threatened by even the slightest display of strength and will seek to either remove it or use it to their advantage. These types of managers usually only engage in self-serving work relationships and will always have a right-hand man or woman that they feign a trustful relationship with, in order to ensure their own survival.

This right-hand man or woman will always ensure that the manager's work is done, so it is in their best interests to build rapport with this person. These types of managers will also be constantly testing the integrity or loyalty of their team to search for rivals, and once spotted will be normally singled out for sabotage with the main goal of either psychological warfare aimed at reducing their effectiveness or complete removal.

Learn to look out for phrases such as "empowerment" or "opportunities for development," because this can be the vocabulary of the consciously inept manager. I once had a line manager who, when appointed as team lead, chose to divide their staff into two groups; those who were in the department the longest and those who were in the department the shortest. He constantly gave the staff who were in the department the shortest "opportunities for development" and heaped false praise on the staff who were present the longest, deeming them "experienced," and created this persona in their heads. This false praise led to the longer serving staff managing the shorter serving staff, while the manager sat back and played no active part in the duties or strategic activities of the team despite being the lead.

One of the main weapons in the armory of a consciously inept manager is the performance appraisal reviews. The manager knows that they alone are key to you receiving either a bonus or potential advancement. They use this as blackmail or as a deterrent to control your perceived insubordination and can also use this as a psychological weapon to make you doubt yourself and your own abilities.

You must remember that a manager in this position, of trying to hold on to their role without being exposed, is the most dangerous animal that you will encounter in the corporate jungle, because nothing is beyond their capabilities in trying to keep you at bay and themselves in a position of power. They will seek to make you lose confidence in yourself, they can spread rumors to sabotage your progression, and can even manipulate business and team objectives to try and set you up for a fall. These managers, however, will always take credit for work done by a team and do not normally give genuine individual praise.

The main defense in this encounter is never to allow them to affect your self-confidence and undermine your natural abilities. You must be aware of how the egos of both combatants can affect these encounters, and getting even, although probably your natural instinct or main goal, is not necessarily the best approach.

You must seek to use all available cover that is present within the environment. You must seek refuge in policy and records.

What I mean by this is that your behavior must always keep in line with regulation and work within organizational rules and policy to ensure that the manager cannot accuse you of poor performance. I'm not suggesting, however, that you work to rule but that you just need to strike a balance in ensuring that governance takes a key focus of your activities.

All encounters must also be documented or minuted to ensure that you have evidence of all interactions that may be used against you. You need to be a step ahead of your manager at every stage, but do not make it overtly visible in your strategy.

One key to success in these interactions is to remove visible emotion from the encounters where possible. This is easier said than done, but if your manager perceives that their efforts are not affecting you, they will more than likely not pursue a method that they deem ineffective.

A key piece of advice here is to never ever refer to your line manager as your "boss," and even in times of peace and harmony in any role or encounter, never let them hear you say the word "boss."

A boss implies a psychological hold or dominance over you by them and is, essentially, a term of subservience and submissiveness that you must never give in to. The same apples to the phrase "immediate superior." Always refer to them as a "manager" or "line manager."

## Winning by Not Winning

In almost every conflict encounter the importance of differentiating winner from loser is often a natural survival trait; everyone wants to be a winner, but what happens when winning is actually a negative.

Let's use the example of the cold war between the United States and the Soviet Union in the 1980s, where winning in this situation meant the obliteration of the entire planet.

Your issue with your manager is, essentially, a small microcosm of wartime survival. Therefore, in an encounter like this, a stalemate can be the best possible outcome for both combatants.

The manager who wishes to force out the employee perceived to be insubordinate ceases the attacks against them, and the employee ceases exposing their manager's ineptitude. Both compromises therefore ensure the effective survival of both combats, because both combatants hold on to their jobs. A Nash equilibrium has been achieved. These, however, are not compromises in the true sense, because each combatant still holds the same motivations of survival, but, rather, a stalemate or indirect compromise has been achieved.

A stalemate is therefore different than a Pyrrhic victory in that no one actually technically achieves formal victory in these situations.

Let's look at how game theory can be utilized here.

This is where game theory and a process known as 'deterrence theory' actually intertwine.

Deterrence theory was coined in the late 20th century by Professor Thomas Schelling, an economist, by highlighting how an inferior force could equal that of their powerful rivals through the presence of a shared powerful possession. This was then applied to nuclear weapons during the cold war era.

In game theory an agent makes choices to ensure their own survival, this is replicated within deterrence theory also. The more powerful force is reluctant to act against the previously labelled 'inferior force' because the element of power has now been leveled, with both sides being an equally dominant power, and therefore engaging in battle would produce no winners. Hence, each side will look to settle on the strategy that causes the least impact and the best outcome for them.

Let's compare this to the corporate world by using the following example:

Gary and his line manager, Kevin, are in a dispute. They both know the implication of continuing and the effect that it will have on their overall careers. They both agree to stand down because they know there are no real winners in this situation and, as we have discussed in Chapter 3, the Nash equilibrium is made to benefit the individual. This is what has happened in the foregoing example, with the added advantage that the Nash equilibrium chosen is actually the best outcome for both, because there is the presence of cooperation.

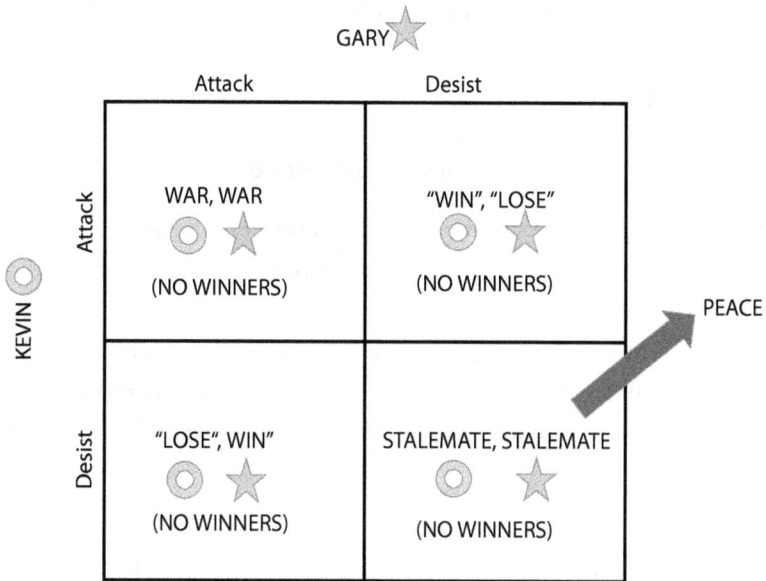

## Psychology of an Ambush

When you suddenly find yourself in the midst of an ambush, a rapid assessment of your options takes place.

You should not seek to engage in direct fire on your opponent at the behest of your imbalanced ego because this will cloud your judgment and the overall rate of success.

Your own motivation for retaliation must be assessed with measured rationality.

Also, the level of imbalance in your ego will affect your recovery after an ambush.

The prospect of revenge will cloud other factors required for your continual survival, so you must learn to control these emotional imbalances.

The first stage, however, in any recovery from an ambush where you have been overpowered is to return your sense of stability and self-confidence. This can arise from small-scale reinforcement techniques that should be carried out in an incremental fashion, each time validating your self-confidence and bringing stability and reassurance back into your mindset. In order to "get back on the horse," as the phrase goes, you must take it in steps and not rush back to battle unnecessarily to satisfy your imbalanced ego in publicly validating your sense of self-purpose.

## Factors of Influence

Despite strategic and tactical awareness and weapon superiority, there are other factors at play that will drastically sway a battle against one side in favor of another.

You must look at the specific situation you find yourself in, and by studying your environment and opponent you will need to establish the following information and see how that can either help win or lose the battle.

- **Safety in Numbers**

The first point is understating the psychology of human beings to feel safety in numbers. Humans seek the presence of other humans and move in herds or packs as a form of protection. These groupings provide a collective defense against predation but can also be used selfishly by many or all of its members.

The "selfish herd theory" was proposed in 1971 by English biologist William D Hamilton, who theorized that individual animals will seek to position themselves at strategic locations within the herd. This is normally at the center of the herd as a higher form of security but can also be near the back or front of the herd in order to aid with escape. So despite having a collective conscious, individuals within the herd will normally look after themselves.

A herd, however, contains omnivorous animals, such as deer and antelope, and the psychology of the pack is not clear-cut. A pack of predatory animals can cause havoc within the animal kingdom, and they can use their skills to work together in a form of collective consciousness in order to achieve their goals, and attacking one member usually incurs the wrath of the others.

This is where you must look to separate them.

*If his forces are united separate them.*

*Sun Tzu (The Art of War)*

Separating packs of office predators is no easy task, the only effective method being to cause fear or dissension within the ranks. All packs, you must remember, are only as strong as their weakest member, so you will need to establish vulnerabilities within each of the members and look for avenues to exploit. This can take some time to do because it will involve many espionage or reconnaissance activities, so if you're restricted by time you should seek to divert their attention to another issue.

Other factors in relation to safety in numbers is the presence of senior management and their interaction with members of this pack. If the senior manager is in favor of this pack, then it will instill a sense of impunity within their behavior, but the inverse is also true, however, because if the senior management is unaware of or indeed indifferent to the pack's behavior, the senior manager becomes an important resource in this quest.

## Other Points to Consider in the Field

You must be conscious of the attention that your activities will draw from other members of the workplace. Missions must therefore be carried out with stealth, because exposure will result in serious damage to you and your brand.

You must remember to conceal footprints and not leave any trace of your presence.

Be careful in choosing allies, because this can sometimes lead to betrayal, and you must be aware of the role of the indigenous population during all these activities; so you must be cautious not to reveal too much about yourself or your operations than what is actually necessary.

Disinformation can also be used sometimes in an attempt to test loyalties, but you must be careful with whom you use it on and at what stages of your activities.

Despite a cautious approach of noncombatants, you must also consider allies even as reinforcement provisions. A strong ally in the corporate world, which is the equivalent of an air strike in a battle, is a trade union. I cannot emphasize how beneficial it is to join a trade union, because this group will always have your back (providing that you are in the right, of course). A trade union is also a deterrent to unscrupulous actions and behaviors of managers.

# CHAPTER 6

# Counterinsurgency Techniques for Organizations (for Natural Ecosystem Balance)

*Salus populi suprema lex*
*(The welfare of the people is the ultimate law.)*

Cicero, Roman Statesman 106–143 BC

Throughout this book we have disused the concept of guerrilla warfare being waged against opponents. We have always defined the opponents as being rivals (or enemies within the workplace such as coworkers or managers) owing to interpersonal relationships and competitive practices that take place each day that can result in conflict.

We have also reviewed potential offensive and defensive strategies aimed at effectively retaliating and defending in these scenarios in order to ensure your survival and have also reviewed the strategies of your opponents. You must understand that organizations do not really express much interest in guerrilla versus guerrilla battles within the workplace; as, they do not see many of them because they happen away from prying eyes and are self-regulated, and they sometimes turn a blind eye because they can be carried out so subtly that senior managers cannot effectively differentiate between a battle or miscommunication as only the actual combatants are aware of this fact. Many corporations see these battles as inevitable and a necessary part of determining the survival of the fittest and the overall effect that it has on the organization's overall performance as long as they don't spill over in full view of the organization. In many cases, as you will see, organizations actually promote competition and it's associated practices.

What if, however, the guerrilla decided to turn their attention to the organization as a whole? What if acts of ambush, sabotage, and corporate terrorism were used against the organization and not the individual? This would have disastrous effects for the organization's image and performance because they would, essentially, be fighting a hidden enemy who knows all their secrets. What if you are the owner or leader of an organization tasked with keeping order and ensuring its optimum performance?

There is also the fear of the insurgency spreading across other departments in accordance with the domino theory, as was feared with the spread of communism in the cold war era.

This is where we need to look at counterinsurgency techniques for organizations in order to restore a sense of balance to the ecosystem, because we have learned that no single species can dominate in the animal kingdom and that therefore the same logic also applies to the business world.

In order to be successful in their counterinsurgency strategies, organizations will also need to understand the distinction between 'guerrilla' and 'anarchist' opponents.

A guerrilla movement implies to the organization that the combatant may have allies or the sympathy and support of the local population and that therefore defeating the guerrillas will not defeat the movement. What if also the morality and cause of the guerrilla is completely incongruous with the business environment? Everyone has a different interpretation of the word guerrilla.

Trying to battle the guerrilla by large-scale bombing or air strikes is inadvisable because this will not only produce civilian casualties, but will also turn the population against the organization, the very thing that you are trying to avoid. Therefore, in order to be effective at fighting guerrillas, organizations must beat them at their own game and deploy corporate counterinsurgency teams into the corporate jungle to locate them.

## Seven Golden Rules

Organizations must understand that they need to follow a set of seven established rules in order to effectively defeat insurgents. These are characterized as follows:

1. **Set Up a Team of Counterinsurgents**

   The first protocol of an organization when seeking to devise an effective counterinsurgency strategy in overcoming guerrillas is to first select a team that is capable of accomplishing the task at hand.

   They should always seek to match the activities and movements of the guerrillas and not appear to make themselves so large as to be easily spotted and exposed. Teams should therefore consist of no more than five members before expanding them based on need.

   Keeping the team small will also control the level of information because any leaks will create impediments to your ultimate progress.

   Team members should be chosen on the basis of skill set, because good communication and perceived neutral people are always more likely to be trusted and viewed as less of a threat to the general population.

   You must remember that in order to locate the guerrillas you must become intertwined with the local population of your organization, so having people who appear trustworthy and neutral will have a positive effect on your operation.

   You must also look at recruiting people who are strong decision makers because decisions will need to be made along the way that will require rapid responses, so someone who is not afraid to make important decisions will be most helpful to your cause.

   The following positions will need to be filled as effectively as possible:

   i) **Guide**

      You must also seek to recruit a member who knows the terrain that the guerrilla operates within. This will be a person who directly interacts with or traverses this terrain on a regular basis and knows the lie of the land. This person will, ideally, be aware of what danger looks like and will seek to safely escort you on your journey.

   ii) **Interpreter**

      You must also seek to recruit a member who knows the culture and language of the local population, such as a recently promoted member of senior management who knows the culture of the local population extremely well. This person will be aware of their plight and behaviors and will obtain key information on the level of sympathy that the population has toward the guerrillas.

This person must be trustworthy, however, because any leaks or natural loyalties to the local population on your activities will scupper your progress and expose your intentions.

### iii) Logistical and Equipment Specialist

This will be a person whose skill set will be gathering information and planning how the aspects of the terrain and level of threat can be channeled into an effective response and what tools are needed to achieve a victory. These tools could be communication requirements or the shelter and weaponry required.

### iv) Medic

A medic is there to stop any superficial casualties incurred by the team turning into something more serious. This person's role is to defuse tension from the local population and suspected guerrillas and bring interactions back to a position of anonymity and calmness. This person should be a natural mediator and should always appear unthreatening.

### v) Leader

The final member of your team who should be appointed as the leader should be someone who holds a position of seniority and commands respect within the organization. This this will give your operation the desired credibility among the local population that you ultimately require. This is the person who will create and direct the strategies. This person's main role initially, however, will be to deflect attention from the local population and guerrillas away from the rest of the team, allowing them to operate covertly. This person is normally installed as key ally within the new regime when the operation is over.

## 2. Locate the Guerrillas

Once you have a team selected and recruited, your next step in the operation should be to locate the guerrillas. You must remember that the team of five that you have selected are not designed to be combatants but scouts who engage in reconnaissance and espionage designed to infiltrate the local population and/or guerrilla faction to gain information on their activities, motivation, and capabilities.

This information will then be used to create an army that carries out the attacks after all the relevant information has been received and a strategy of attack methodically determined.

When first seeking to locate the guerrillas, you will need to understand the lie of the land, and this is where your guide will be effective. Guerrillas will always prefer to battle on what is deemed 'favorable ground,' which is essentially terrain that affords them the most cover, but in many situations this is not possible, and they will have to intertwine with the local population to engage in battle. This is what is termed 'unfavorable ground' or 'urban warfare.'

In order for the guerrilla to be effective at urban warfare, they must have the support of the local population, without which they are exposed.

The guerrilla and the local inhabitant will always be hard to distinguish between, so extreme care must be taken in making assumptions without the facts.

Your presence within the local environment will also cause concern and anxiety to the local population, so you must seek to make your presence as less intimidating as possible. You are there to gain their trust and to elicit important information from them on their loyalties or the whereabouts of the guerrillas.

On favorable ground, guerrillas will need to set up camps in order to adhere to their most basic needs: shelter, sleep, and sustenance. These camps will often be located strategically near a water source, so attention must be paid to the presence of eating or resting activities within the corporate office.

Understanding who eats with whom and where they eat is critical to the counterinsurgency force because people who disappear off-site together at lunchtime may be possible candidates. You must be extremely careful however not to unfairly profile or label inhabitants as being guerrillas, because without solid evidence this will ultimately backfire on you.

You must learn to interpret signs of guerrilla presence such as tracks or disturbed vegetation or animal life. Watching the behavior of animals is also a telling sign that guerrillas are present. In the corporate world a civilian will always act anxious when a guerrilla is present, and these subtle signs must be homed in on and documented.

Therefore, when seeking to locate the guerrillas it is of critical importance that you seek to win over the local population. This is where your interpreter will be useful because they will be able to communicate the often subtle information conveyed by the local population on their motivations and plight.

## Propaganda

You must also be aware that the guerrilla, in order to effectively win over the local population, instills their own brand of propaganda. You must seek to break this hold that they have over the general population by instilling your own form of propaganda. Your own propaganda is not necessarily an attempt at brainwashing but merely an operation to spread the truth about certain activities that may have been misinterpreted by the local population and exploited by the guerrilla to brainwash the local population.

You must also offer a better resolution to the problems faced by the local population than the offerings that have been promoted to them by the guerrillas so you must seek to create prosperity in their lives and strive to improve their ultimate way of life.

This can be done by means of promises of promotion and restructuring with the goal of conferring more autonomy or positions of seniority on them. You must be careful, however, not to confuse these with bribes because the local population will be very wary of these types of offerings. The local population will have a high sense of morality and will respond only to information or promises that they deem truthful and that will bring change to the population as a whole. You will always find self-serving members of the local population, however, but rewarding the few and not the many will not sway the entire population or deter the guerrillas.

3. **Set Up Base and Logistical Hub for Operations**

Once you have won over the local population, you have easily exposed the guerrilla who have now been located. You must now, however, plan your attack strategies with the main goal of zero collateral damage. This is where your logistics and equipment specialist will be effective because they will advise on the weaponry and communication equipment required to carry out the attack.

The position of the guerrillas is of critical importance, and also their level of exposure, and you must ascertain whether they are positioned too close to the local population, making a shot on target more risky, in which case you must look at ways to lure or bait them out of hiding. The techniques of flushing and baiting discussed in the previous chapter are of great use here.

This information must all be relayed back to the central command so that a team of active combatants can enter the environment.

4. **Wipe Out Insurgents (Battle)**

Once the guerrillas have been located and exposed, this is where they must be eliminated. You must seek to establish whether you need or want to have them captured alive and imprisoned or eliminated completely.

From experience the best way is to capture them alive so that the local population will be forever reminded of the consequences of attacking the corporation.

The organization can choose the active combatants from an army already in place in the form of HR. You must remember that once a guerrilla is exposed, they are not effective in any further battle.

The organization may also seek to use mercenaries for this task, those being people who are not directly connected to the organization, such as law enforcement (depending on the severity) or independent bodies set up to deal with conflict resolution and punishment. This will reduce the focus on the organization as being the aggressor.

5. **Local Elections and Installment of New Government (New Job Roles)**

Once you have eliminated the guerrillas, you will now need to fulfil your promises to the local population that you made earlier in the campaign in return for their loyalty and support. You must seek to restructure their environment, create opportunities for advancement, and instill a general sense of optimism in their daily lives. You are now showing them the benefits of obedience to corporate policy and will deter any future mutinies that may arise.

6. **Support New Government (Funding; Budgetary)**

Once you have restructured their department and created opportunities for advancement, you must seek to remove any external impediments to their departmental success. You must take a hands-on role in determining their new successful operations in order to ensure that the department is productive, and so you may need to make other departments more receptive or productive to ensure their collective survival.

7. **Withdrawal**

Once you have removed these external impediments wherever possible and created a sense of autonomy and high motivation in the new department, you must now step off. You never truly step away completely, but you must remember that your continued presence may imply to the local population a sense of distrust and may also be a reminder to potential disenfranchised elements that may still remain whom you are unaware of. Hence, you must learn when and how to step off and you must make an effective exit strategy a priority, but always keep a watchful eye on the operations. This can be done by installing the leader of your reconnaissance team into one of the positions of power. They are respected by the population and are also loyal to you, so they would make an ideal fit.

Organizations that seek to put profit before people will always struggle to influence the natural ecosystem balance. While the pursuit of profit is a natural goal of corporate games, it can be achieved only via collaboration and interdependences of the players involved.

Competition that is too intense within an environment will lead to greater losses to all involved. The organization must strive to take a more influential position in regulating the individual competition and seek to promote collaboration at every turn. This will ensure a much more productive environment for all.

*Aut viam inveniam aut faciam*
(I shall either find a way or make one.)

Hannibal, Carthaginian military commander, 247–183 BC

# Bibliography

## Chapter 1

Chapter introduction quote: Cicero, Roman statesman (106–104 BC).

"Principals of Population," by economist Robert Malthus in 1798 (ISBN 978-0-521075930).

"The Origin of the Species" 1859 Charles Darwin (ISBN 978-0-00-790223-1)

Jane Goodall mentioned but not referenced.

Mark Berhoff, "The Emotional Lives of Animals" (ISBN 978-1-57731-629-9) mentioned but not referenced.

## Chapter 2

Chapter introduction quote: Ovid, Roman Poet (43 BC–17 AD).

Facts on animal naming and figures checked using Encyclopaedia Britannica as a reference https://www.britannica.com/.

Sun Tzu (The Art of War) (ISBN 978-0-9811626-1-4).

National Health Service's (NHS) website: www.nhs.uk https://www.nhs.uk/conditions/antisocial-personality-disorder/.

Niccollo Machiavelli "The Prince" (ISBN 978-0-140-44915-0).

Mayo clinic (www.mayoclinic.org) https://www.mayoclinic.org/diseases-conditions/narcissistic-personality-disorder/symptoms-causes/syc-20366662

The Cambridge Dictionary, https://dictionary.cambridge.org/.

Sigmund Freud, "The Ego and the ID" (ISBN -10 1451537239, ISBN 13: 978-1451537239).

"Big Five Personality Factors, The Psycholexical Approach to Personality," by Boele de Raad (ISBN 0889372365) used as reference but not quoted.

Paul Levy, "Levy Flight" referenced but not quoted.

"Henri Poincare—Impatient Genius" by Ferdinand Verhulst, (ISBN 978-1-4614-2406-2) used as reference but not quoted.

"The Essence of Chaos" by Edward Lorenz (ISBN 0-203-21458-7).

# Chapter 3

Chapter introduction quote: Gottfried Leibniz, German Philosopher (1646-1716).

Game Theory and Strategy by Philip D. Straffin (ISBN 0-88385-600-X) used as a reference but not quoted.

Evolution and the Theory of Games by John Maynard Smyth (ISBN 0-521-28884.3).

The Dove and Hawk images icons used in chapter 3 have been obtained from Flaticon.com – source: https://www.flaticon.com/free-icon/dove_92009?term=dove&page=1&position=3

https://www.flaticon.com/free-icon/hawk-bird-animal-shape_47294?term=hawk&page=1&position=1

# Chapter 4

Chapter introduction quote: Publilius Syrus, Latin writer born in Syria (85–43 BC).

Research Paper Kidd, A. H., H. T. Kelley, and R. M. Kidd. 1983. "Personality Characteristics of Horse, Turtle, Snake and Bird Owners." *Psychological Reports*, 52, pp. 719–29. https://journals.sagepub.com/doi/abs/10.2466/pr0.1983.52.3.719?journalCode=prxa#articlePermissionsContainer.

Referenced study by Professor Richard Wiseman from the University of Herefordshire.

Referenced study by Sadahiko Nakajima, a psychologist at Japan's Kwansei Gakuin University.

Referenced 2019–2020 APPA (American Pet Products Association) National Pet Owners' survey.

Cambridge English Dictionary, https://dictionary.cambridge.org/.

Joseph Wolf Psychiatrist credited with discovery of "Systematic Desensitisation."

Leon Festinger credited with discovery of "Cognitive Dissonance."

Sigmund Fraud credited with discovery of "Defence Mechanism Theory."

Oregon State University and Journal of Experimental Gerontology and Caroline Alwin for the "Centre for Health Aging," https://www.npr.org/sections/health-shots/2014/09/22/349875448/best-to-not-sweat-the-small-stuff-because-it-could-kill-you.

British Medical Journal, https://www.nhs.uk/news/mental-health/worried-to-death-distress-linked-to-early-death/.

www.Macmilliandictionary.com.

www.merriam-webster.com.

Chapter close out quote: Albert Einstein.

# Chapter 5

Chapter introduction quote: Publius Flavius Vegetius Renatus, Roman Writer, 4th century BC.

"The Art of War" by Sun Tzu (ISBN 978-0-9811626-1-4).

www.verywellmind.com

Ernesto "Che" Guevara—Guerrilla Warfare (ISBN 9562915719).

*Mao Tse Tung Quote*—On Guerillas Warfare (ISBN 13: 978-0-486-44376-8, ISBN 10: 0-486-44376-0).

Science of Freezing, www.psychologytoday.com.

Description of Procrastination from www.mindtools.com.

Definition of Hesitation—Cambridge Dictionary, https://dictionary.cambridge.org/.

UPMC department of neurosurgery, https://share.upmc.com/2015/07/the-science-behind-procrastination/.

Mao Tse Tung—On Guerillas Warfare (ISBN 13: 978-0-486-44376-8, ISBN 10: 0-486-44376-0).

Friedrich Nietzsche (Austrian Philosopher) quote.

British naturalist Henry Walter Bates—Bastian Mimicry (Textbook of Animal Behaviour F.B. Mandel (ISBN 8120351487) used as a reference but not quoted).

German naturalist Fritz Muller—Mullerian Mimicry Textbook of animal behaviour F.B. Mandel (ISBN 8120351487) used as a reference but not quoted).

American naturalist, Abbot Handerson Thayer—Thayers Law quoted but not referenced.

US General Ricardo Sanchez—Flypaper Theory.

Gaslighting Definition from Encyclopaedia Britannica. A report published in 2010 by the General accounting office (GAO), https://www.gao.gov/new.items/d05687.pdf

British Daily Mirror article, https://www.mirror.co.uk/news/world-news/british-army-fired-46-million-5475716.

US Department of Defence's Pharmacoeconomic centre, https://www.ib-times.com/medicating-our-troops-oblivion-prescription-drugs-said-be-endangering-us-soldiers-1572217.

International Association of Chiefs of police in the USA as part of an initiative with CNA, the Department of Justice Office of Community Oriented Policing Services (COPS), and the International Association of Chiefs of Police (IACP), https://www.theiacp.org/sites/default/files/2018-08/IACP_Ambush_Fact_Sheet.pdf.

Late 20th Century psychologist Paul Ekman quoted but not referenced National Academy of Sciences, https://www.forbes.com/sites/brucelee/2017/09/09/here-are-the-27-different-human-emotions-according-to-a-study/.

Modernised Victor Hugo quote from "Villemain."

www.Globalsecurity.org used as reference but not quoted.

U.S. Army Counterinsurgency Warrior Handbook – Department of the Army ISBN 1493016237, 9781493016235 used as reference but not quoted

The Counter Insurgency Manual—Lehroy Thompson (ISBN 978-1-84832-826-6) used as reference but not quoted.

A History of Jungle warfare—Brian Perrett (ISBN 1473847532) used as reference but not quoted.

# Chapter 6

Chapter introduction quote: Cicero, Roman Statesman (106–143 BC).

The Counter Insurgency Manual—Lehroy Thompson (ISBN 978-1-84832-826-6) used as reference but not quoted.

A History of Jungle warfare—Brian Perrett (ISBN 1473847532) used as reference but not quoted.

Ernesto "Che" Guevara – Guerrilla Warfare (ISBN 9562915719).

Mao Tse Tung—On Guerrilla Warfare (ISBN 13: 978-0-486-44376-8, ISBN 10: 0-486-44376-0).

Chapter close out quote: Hannibal, Carthaginian military commander, (247–183 BC).

# About the Author

*K.F. Dochartaigh* has worked in the corporate world for over 20 years in various capacities at senior levels in both the private and the public sectors and even ran his own company some time ago.

He graduated in 2007 and is member of numerous professional chartered bodies. He has been working since he was 16 years old and has been in industry ever since in which he has been responsible for the creation and strategic management of multibillion dollar infrastructure and built environment supply chains. But continues to be fascinated by the everyday actions, behaviors, and motivations of people in the rat race.

The author has documented all the knowledge that he has learned in order to help both people at the start of their careers and those who have hit a wall with their current position at any stage in their careers.

He also has a keen interest in the history of warfare, specifically the effects of warfare on human psychology and the politics at play behind the scenes on the international stage.

Also being an animal lover and wildlife conservation advocate Mr. Dochartaigh has combined his passions under one umbrella to develop and present this piece of work.

# Formal Permissions Obtained for Quotations >100 Words

1. National Health Service's (NHS; https://www.nhs.uk/conditions/antisocial-personality-disorder/)
2. Mayo clinic (https://www.mayoclinic.org/diseases- conditions/narcissistic-personality-disorder/symptoms-causes/ syc-20366662)
3. Research Paper Kidd, A.H., Kelley, H.T., & Kidd, R.M. (1983). "Personality Characteristics of Horse, Turtle, Snake and Bird Owners." *Psychological Reports* 52, pp. 719-29. https://journals.sagepub.com/doi/abs/10.2466/pr0.1983.52.3.719?journalCode=prxa#articlePermissionsContainer

## Picture Permissions and Acknowledgements

*Amphibians*

Salamanders (*Caudata*)

https://commons.wikimedia.org/wiki/File:Fire_Salamander.jpg
This file is licensed under the Creative Commons Attribution 2.0 Generic license.
Photographer: William Warby (https://www.flickr.com/people/26782864@N00)

Frogs (*Anura*)

https://www.pexels.com/photo/green-blue-yellow-and-orange-frog-on-green-leaf-76957/
Photographer: Pixabay (https://www.pexels.com/@pixabay)

Caecilians (*Apoda*)

https://commons.wikimedia.org/wiki/File:A_large_caecilian_(14658344987).jpg

### Reptiles

Snakes (*Serpentes*)

Lizards (*Squamata*)

Turtles (*Testudines*)

Caiman (*Crocodilians*)

### Birds

Parrots (*Psittaciformes*)

Songbirds (*Passeriformes*)

https://www.pexels.com/photo/close-up-photo-of-brown-bird-2570085/
Photographer: Miri (https://www.pexels.com/@anacardia)

**Pheasants, Chickens, Peacocks, and Turkeys (Galliformes)**

Peacock

https://www.pexels.com/photo/blue-and-green-peacock-638738/
Photographer: Naushil Ansari (https://www.pexels.com/@naushil-ansari-151720)

**Birds of Prey**

Falcons (*Falconiformes*)

https://www.pexels.com/photo/falcon-perched-on-tree-1887830/
Photographer: Frans Van Heerden (https://www.pexels.com/@frans-van-heerden-201846)

**Eagles and Vultures (Accipitriformes)**

Eagles

https://www.pexels.com/photo/black-and-white-eagle-73825/
Photographer: Pixabay (https://www.pexels.com/@pixabay)

Vultures

https://www.pexels.com/photo/animal-avian-beak-bird-460857/
Photographer: Pixabay (https://www.pexels.com/@pixabay)

**Creepy Crawlies (Arthropods)**

Spiders (*Arachnids*)

https://www.pexels.com/photo/brown-jumping-spider-on-green-leaf-plant-973389/

Photographer: Angeli Ann Dinsay (https://www.pexels.com/@angeli-ann-dinsay-359166)

Scorpions (*Arachnids*)

https://commons.wikimedia.org/wiki/File:Scorpion_Alacranes_Gueros.jpg
This file is licensed under the Creative Commons Attribution-Share Alike 4.0 International license.
Photographer: Dominic Gagnon (https://commons.wikimedia.org/w/index.php?title=User:Dominic_Gagnon&action=edit&redlink=)

Centipedes and Millipedes (*Myriapods*)

https://www.pexels.com/photo/black-and-brown-millipede-on-a-green-and-brown-branch-63657/
Photographer: Pixabay (https://www.pexels.com/@pixabay)

Ants (*Formicidae*)

https://www.pexels.com/photo/close-up-photography-of-red-ant-on-green-leaf-1104974/
Photographer: Egor Kamelev (https://www.pexels.com/@ekamelev)

Bees (*Apoidea*)

https://www.pexels.com/photo/honeycomb-close-up-detail-honey-bee-56876/
Photographer: Pixabay (https://www.pexels.com/@pixabay)

Wasps and Hornets (*Vespa*)

https://www.pexels.com/photo/gravid-yellow-jacket-wasp-closeup-photography-928972/
Photographer: David Hablützel (https://www.pexels.com/@umsiedlungen)

Mosquitos and Flies (*Diptera*)

https://www.pexels.com/photo/mosquito-biting-on-skin-2382223/
Photographer: Jimmy Chan (https://www.pexels.com/@jimbear)

Butterflies and Moths (Including Caterpillars) (*Lepidoptera*)

https://www.pexels.com/photo/female-monarch-butterfly-perching-on-red-petal-flower-1557208/
Photographer: Tinthia Clemant (https://www.pexels.com/@tinthia-clemant-16649)

## *Molluscs*

Snails and Slugs (*Gastropods*)

https://www.pexels.com/photo/white-and-brown-shell-snail-on-green-leaf-53203/
Photographer: Pixabay (https://www.pexels.com/@pixabay)

## *Fish*

Cartilaginous Fish (*Chondrichthyes*)

Sharks (*Selachimorpha*)

https://www.pexels.com/photo/photo-of-shark-near-corals-3311083/
Photographer: Photographer: Pixabay (https://www.pexels.com/@pixabay)

Rays (*Batoidea*)

https://www.pexels.com/photo/stingray-under-water-2832643/
Photographer: Magda Ehlers (https://www.pexels.com/@magda-ehlers-pexels)

Bony Fish (*Osteichthyes*)

Piranha (*Serrasalmidae*)

https://commons.wikimedia.org/wiki/File:Gfp-vicious-red-bellied-piranha.jpg

This file has been released explicitly into the public domain by its author, using the Creative Commons Public Domain Dedication.

This file may be used for any purpose including unrestricted redistribution, commercial use, and modification.

Photographer: Yinan Chen (https://www.goodfreephotos.com/)

## Mammals

Rodents (*Rodentia*)

https://www.pexels.com/photo/waiting-hidden-mouse-95399/
Photographer: Shashank Kumawat (https://www.pexels.com/@shashank)

Bats (*Chiroptera*)

https://www.pexels.com/photo/selective-focus-photo-of-black-bat-on-brown-stone-3261020/
Photographer: HitchHike (https://www.pexels.com/@hitchhike-1709677)

Shrews and Hedgehogs (*Eulipotyphla*)

https://commons.wikimedia.org/wiki/File:Crocidura_russula_shrew.jpg

This work has been released into the **public domain** by its author, **Sjonge** (https://en.wikipedia.org/wiki/User:Sjonge) at **English Wikipedia**. This applies worldwide.

In some countries this may not be legally possible; if so:

Sjonge grants anyone the right to use this work **for any purpose**, without any conditions, unless such conditions are required by law. Public domainPublic domainfalsefalse.

## Sloths and Anteaters (Pilosa)

Sloths

https://commons.wikimedia.org/wiki/File:Brown-throated_three-toed_sloth_female.JPG

This file is licensed under the Creative Commons Attribution-Share Alike 3.0 Unported license.

Photographer: Sharp Photography (https://www.sharpphotography.co.uk/)

## Anteaters

https://commons.wikimedia.org/wiki/File:Anteater_2016.jpg

This file is licensed under the Creative Commons Attribution-Share Alike 4.0 International license.

Photographer: RedGazelle15 (https://commons.wikimedia.org/w/index.php?title=User:RedGazelle15&action=edit&redlink=1)

## *Apes and Monkeys (Primates)*

### Gorillas

https://www.pexels.com/photo/gorilla-beside-brown-rock-913652/

Photographer: Chris Carter (https://www.pexels.com/@chriscarterux)

### Chimpanzees

https://commons.wikimedia.org/wiki/File:Pan_troglodytes_32zz.jpg

This file is licensed under the Creative Commons Attribution-Share Alike 4.0 International license.

Photographer: David Stang. First published at ZipcodeZoo.com

### Monkeys

https://www.pexels.com/photo/white-and-beige-monkey-145947/

Photographer: Flickr (https://www.pexels.com/@flickr)

### Lemur

https://commons.wikimedia.org/wiki/File:Crowned_lemur_(Eulemur_coronatus)_female_head.jpg

This file is licensed under the Creative Commons Attribution-Share Alike 4.0 International license.

Photographer: Sharp Photography (https://www.sharpphotography.co.uk/)


## Bonobos

https://commons.wikimedia.org/wiki/File:Apeldoorn_Apenheul_zoo_Bonobo.jpg

This file is licensed under the Creative Commons Attribution-Share Alike 3.0 Unported license.

Attribution: Natataek at English Wikivoyage

Photographer: Natataek (https://en.wikivoyage.org/wiki/User:Natataek)


## Gibbons

https://commons.wikimedia.org/wiki/File:Gibbon_%C3%A0_favoris_roux_femelle_DSCF3618.jpg

This file is licensed under the Creative Commons Attribution-Share Alike 4.0 International license.

Photographer: Musicaline (https://commons.wikimedia.org/wiki/User:Musicaline)


## *Hoofed Animals* (Ungulates)

https://commons.wikimedia.org/wiki/File:Okapi-Wald1.png

This work has been released into the **public domain** by its author, **Nachbarnebenan at German Wikipedia**. This applies worldwide.

In some countries this may not be legally possible; if so:

Nachbarnebenan (https://de.wikipedia.org/wiki/Benutzer:Nachbarnebenan) grants anyone the right to use this work **for any purpose**, without any conditions, unless such conditions are required by law. Public domain


## *Elephants* (Elephantidae)

https://www.pexels.com/photo/view-of-elephant-in-water-247431/

Photographer: Pixabay (https://www.pexels.com/@pixabay)

### Meat-Eating Predators (Carnivora)

Tigers (*Panthera tigris*)

https://commons.wikimedia.org/wiki/File:Sumatran_Tiger_(9122811106).jpg
This file is made available under the Creative Commons CC0 1.0 Universal Public Domain Dedication.
The person who associated a work with this deed has dedicated the work to the public domain by waiving all of their rights to the work worldwide under copyright law, including all related and neighboring rights, to the extent allowed by law. You can copy, modify, distribute, and perform the work, even for commercial purposes, all without asking permission.
Photographer: Bernard Spragg. NZ (https://www.flickr.com/people/88123769@N02) from Christchurch, New Zealand

Jaguars (*Panthera onca*)

https://commons.wikimedia.org/wiki/File:Jaguar_(Panthera_onca_palustris)_male_Rio_Negro_2.JPG
This file is licensed under the Creative Commons Attribution-Share Alike 4.0 International license.
Photographer: Sharp Photography (https://www.sharpphotography.co.uk/)

### Levy Flight

https://commons.wikimedia.org/wiki/File:LevyFlight.svg
The copyright holder of this work released this work into the public domain. This applies worldwide.
In some countries, this may not be legally possible; if so:
I grant anyone the right to use this work for any purpose, without any conditions, unless such conditions are required by law.
Author: User: PAR

### Flow Chart

https://commons.wikimedia.org/wiki/File:Oversimplified_flow_chart_for_editing.png

## Book Cover

www.istockphoto.com – credit: 'Freder'

https://www.istockphoto.com/photo/eyes-of-the-tiger-gm171587129-22066010?clarity=false

https://www.istockphoto.com/portfolio/freder?assettype=image&mediat ype=photography&sort=best

# Index

Accipitriformes, 46
Active color matching, 147
African bonobo (*Pan paniscus*), 93
African forest elephant (*Loxodonta cyclotis*), 90
African honeybee—(*Apis mellifera*) Hybrid, 60
After work drinks, 109
Aggressive mimicry, 141–142
Alcohol, 109
Alwin, Caroline, 128
Amazonian giant centipede (*Scolopendra gigantean*), 46
Ambition, 132–133
Ambush
    psychology of, 197–198
    strategy, 163–164
    tactics, 164–168
Amphibians, 22–29
    caecilians (Apoda), 28–29
    frogs and toads (Anura), 25–27
    mushroom-tongued salamanders (Bolitoglossa), 24–25
    salamanders (Caudata), 23–24
Anger, 184–186
Animals' behavior, 10, 13, 22, 24–26, 28–30, 32, 33, 35, 41, 44, 52, 55, 62, 63, 65, 76, 81, 82, 88, 91, 94, 98, 99, 100, 101, 102, 106
Anopheles albimanus, 65
Anthropomorphism, 9
Antisocial personality disorders (APD), 14–15, 18
Anxiety, 182–183
APD. *See* Antisocial personality disorders
Aposematism, 156
Area ambush, 166
Assassin caterpillar (*Lonomia obliqua*), 67

Awkwardness, 183
Aye Aye (*Daubentonia madagascariensis*), 95

Baiting, 144–146
Bates, Henry Walter, 142
Batesian mimicry, 142–143
Bekoff, Marc, 9
Birds, 39–46
    parrots (Psittaciformes), 40–42
    pheasants, peacocks, chickens, and turkeys (Galliformes), 44–46
    songbirds: (Passennes), 42–44
Birds of prey, 46–51
    eagles and vultures (Accipitriformes), 48–51
    falcons (Falconiformes), 46–48
Black caiman (*Melanosuchus niger*), 37–39
Black rats: (*Rattus rattus*—Invasive species), 76
Blue spotted ribbon tail ray (*Taeniura lymma*), 74
Bonobos, 92–93
Bony fish (Osteichthyes), 75–77
Booby traps, 176, 177
Brazilian wandering spider *Phoneutria fera,* 53
Brazilian yellow scorpion (*Tityus serrulatus*), 54
*British Medical Journal, 129*
Brown-throated sloth (*Bradypus variegatus*), 86
Bull shark (*Carcharhinus leucas*), 72
Bullet ant (*Paraponera clavata*), 58
Bully, identifying and dealing, 187–189
Bullying, 187
Butterfly Effect, 102

C/U-shaped ambush, 172
Calls and false alarms, 144

*Cambridge Dictionary*, 18, 125
Camouflage, 146
  background color matching,
    146–147
  countershading, 148
  disruptive coloration, 147–148
  motion dazzle, 149
  self-decoration, 149
Cardinal payoff, 116
Cartilaginous fish (*Chondrichthyes*),
  71–75
Central American bird of prey, 49
Centre for Health Aging
  Research, 128
Chaos theory, 102
"Che" Guevara, Ernesto, 137
Chumming, shark, 73
Cognitive dissonance, 126–127
Collateral damage, 178
Comrey, Andrew, 21
Consciously inept managers, 192–195
Cooperative and noncooperative
  games, 112–113
COPS. *See* Department of Justice
  Office of Community
  Oriented Policing Services
Corporate jungle
  corporate ladder11–12
  fruits of the jungle, 11
  jungle, 3–5
  rainforest layers
    security layer, 7–8
    service layer, 8–9
    specialist layer, 9–11
    strategic layer, 8
Corporate ladder11–12
Corporate pigeonholing, 132
Corporate psychological warfare, 136
  deception, 141
  deflect, 140
  freeze, 138–140
  retreat, 137
  surrender, 140–141
Corporate sabotage, 176
Corporate social responsibility (CSR),
  6–7
Corporate terrorism, 177–178
Corporate values, 6
Coworker, 112

Creepy crawlies, 51–70
  ants (Formicidea), 57–59
  bees (Apoidea), 59–62
  butterflies, moths and caterpillars
    (Lepidoptera), 65–68
  centipedes, Millipedes (Myriapods),
    55–57
  mosquitos and flies (Diptera),
    63–65
  scorpions, 54–55
  snails and slugs (Gastropods),
    68–70
  spiders, scorpions (Arachnids),
    52–54
  wasps and hornets (Vespa), 62–63
CSR. *See* Corporate social
  responsibility

Darwin, Charles, 2, 11
Defending coworkers, 190
Deimatic behavior, 157
Deliberate ambush, 163
Denial, 127
Department of Justice Office of
  Community Oriented Policing
  Services (COPS), 164
Deterrence theory, 196
Dho Gaza, 47
Diamond-shaped ambush, 173–174
Digman, John, 21
Disgust, 183
Displacement, 128
Driving, 179–180
Dunning, David, 192
Dunning–Kruger effect, 192

Eastern lowland gorilla (*Gorilla
  beringei graueri*), 91
Effective counterinsurgency methods,
  168–175
Ego, 18, 19
  turtles, 36
Egocentric, 14
Einstein, Albert, 133
Ekman, Paul, 181
E-mail, 108, 150
*The Emotional Lives of Animals*, 9
Emotions, animals, 10
*Encyclopaedia Britannica,* 152

Engaging hr, benefits and limitations
of, 189–190
Envy, 183–184
Espionage, 160–161
Ethology, 9
Evolutionary game theory, 117–120
Executioner wasp (*Polistes carnifex*),
62

Facebook, 110
Factors of influence, 198
Falconiformes, 46
False flags, 179
False movements and decoys, 151
False retreats, 151
Far ambush, 165
Favorable/unfavorable ground, 159,
205
Fear, 182–183
Festinger, Leon, 126
Fight, 158
Fish, 70–77
Flushing, 180
Football, 112
French Revolution (1789–1799), 2
Freud, Sigmund, 19, 127
Fruits of the jungle, 11
Funnel trap, 25

Gaslighting, 152–153
Geographic cone snail (*Conus
geographus*), 69
Ghillie suits, 149
Giant anteater (*Myrmecophaga
tridactyla*), 86
Gibbons, 93
Goldberg, Lewis, 21
Golden poison dart frog (*Phyllobates
terribilis*), 27
Goldilocks zone, 110
Goodall, Jane, 9
Gorillas, 91
Green peacock (*Pavo muticus*),
45–46
Guatemalan black howler monkey
(*Alouatta pigra*), 94

Hairy-legged vampire bats (*Diphylla
ecaudata*), 80

Hamilton, William D, 198
Harpy eagle (*Harpia harpyja*), 49
Hawk/Dove, 118
Hesitation, 139
Hierarchies, 191–195
Honest signaling, 155–156
Honey, bees, 60
Human emotions, 181–186
Hyacinth macaw (*Anodorhynchus
hyacinthinus*), 41

IACP. *See* International Association of
Chiefs of Police
ID, 19
Importance of compasses, 130
Indirect ambushes, 164
Infiltration, 160–161
Infrasound and ultrasound, 150
Instagram, 110
Instinct versus learned behaviors,
125–126
International Association of Chiefs of
Police (IACP), 164
I-shaped ambush, 166

Jaguars (Panthera onca), 98–99
Japan's Kwansei Gakuin
University, 122
*Journal of Experimental
Gerontology, 128*
Jungle, 3–5, 122–125

Khedda traps, 90
King vulture (Sarcoramphus papa),
50
Know your environment
cooperative and noncooperative
games, 112–113
evolutionary game theory, 117–120
prisoner's dilemma, 114–116
social dilemma, 116–117
unnatural selection, 104–112
game theory, 111–112
Know your opponent
African bonobo (Pan paniscus), 93
African forest elephant (Loxodonta
cyclotis), 90
African honeybee—(Apis mellifera)
Hybrid, 60

Know your opponent (*contd.*)
  amazonian giant centipede
    (Scolopendra gigantean), 46
  amphibians, 22–29
    salamanders (Caudata), 23–24
    mushroom-tongued salamanders
      (Bolitoglossa), 24–25
    frogs and toads (Anura), 25–27
    caecilians (Apoda), 28–29
  anopheles albimanus, 65
  assassin caterpillar (Lonomia
    obliqua), 67
  aye (Daubentonia
    madagascariensis), 95
  birds, 39–46
    parrots (Psittaciformes), 40–42
    pheasants, peacocks, chickens,
      and turkeys (Galliformes),
      44–46
    songbirds: (Passennes), 42–44
  birds of prey, 46–51
    eagles and vultures
      (Accipitriformes), 48–51
    falcons (Falconiformes), 46–48
  black caiman (Melanosuchus niger),
    37–39
  black rats: (Rattus rattus—Invasive
    species), 76
  blue spotted ribbon tail ray
    (Taeniura lymma), 74
  bonobos, 92–93
  bony fish (Osteichthyes), 75–77
  brazilian wandering spider
    Phoneutria fera, 53
  brazilian yellow scorpion (Tityus
    serrulatus), 54
  brown-throated sloth (Bradypus
    variegatus), 86
  bull shark (Carcharhinus leucas), 72
  bullet ant (Paraponera clavata), 58
  cartilaginous fish (Chondrichthyes),
    71–75
  creepy crawlies, 51–70
    ants (Formicidea), 57–59
    bees (Apoidea), 59–62
    butterflies, moths and caterpillars
      (Lepidoptera), 65–68
    centipedes, Millipedes
      (Myriapods), 55–57

    mosquitos and flies (Diptera),
      63–65
    scorpions, 54–55
    snails and slugs (Gastropods),
      68–70
    spiders, scorpions (Arachnids),
      52–54
    wasps and hornets (Vespa), 62–63
  eastern lowland gorilla (Gorilla
    beringei graueri), 91
  ego, 19
  executioner wasp (Polistes
    carnifex), 62
  fish, 70–77
  geographic cone snail (Conus
    geographus), 69
  giant anteater (Myrmecophaga
    tridactyla), 86
  gibbons, 93
  golden poison dart frog (Phyllobates
    terribilis), 27
  gorillas, 91
  green peacock (Pavo muticus),
    45–46
  guatemalan black howler monkey
    (Alouatta pigra), 94
  hairy-legged vampire bats (Diphylla
    ecaudata), 80
  harpy eagle (Harpia harpyja), 49
  hyacinth macaw (Anodorhynchus
    hyacinthinus), 41
  ID, 19
  jaguars (Panthera onca), 98–99
  king vulture (Sarcoramphus papa), 50
  lemurs, 94–95
  Malaysian water monitor (Varanus
    salvator), 33–34
  mammals, 77–96
    apes and monkeys (Primates),
      90–96
    bats (Chiroptera), 80–81
    elephants (Elephantidae), 89–90
    hoofed animals (Ungulates),
      87–88
    meat-eating predators
      (Carnivora), 96–102
    rodents (Rodentia), 77–79
    shrews and hedgehogs
      (Eulipotyphla), 81–83

sloths and anteaters (Pilosa), 83–86
Mata Mata Turtle (Chelus fimbriata), 35–36
okapi (Okapia johnstoni), 87–88
peregrine falcon (Falco Peregrinus), 47
personality, 21–22
red-bellied piranhas (Pygocentrus nattereri), 76
reptiles, 29–39
    crocodiles, alligators, and caimans (crocodilians), 36–39
    snakes and lizards (squamites), 30–34
    turtles and tortoises (testudines), 34–36
siamang (Symphalangus syndactylus), 93
South American rattlesnake (Crotalus durissus), 31
sumatran tigers (Panthera tigris sondaica), 96–98
superego, 20–21
the central chimpanzee/ tschego (Pan troglodytes troglodytes), 92
thomson's caecilian (Caecilia Thompsoni), 29
thor's hero shrew (Scutisorex thori), 82
vogelkop superb bird-of-paradise (Lophorina niedda), 43
vultures, 49–51
Know yourself
    ambition, 132–133
    cognitive dissonance, 126–127
    denial, 127
    displacement, 128
    importance of compasses, 130
    instinct versus learned behaviors, 125–126
    jungle, 122–125
    reaction formation, 128
    repression, 127
    respect, 131–132
    stockholm syndrome, 127–128
    stress, 128–130
    success and enemies, 130–131
    systematic desensitization, 126
Kruger, Justin, 192

Lemurs, 94–95
Levy, Paul, 100
Lorenz, Edwards, 102
L-shaped ambush, 168, 169

Machiavelli, Niccolo, 16
Machiavellian, 14, 16, 124
Malaysian water monitor (Varanus salvator), 33–34
Malthus, Robert, 1–2
Mammals, 77–96
    apes and monkeys (Primates), 90–96
    bats (Chiroptera), 80–81
    elephants (Elephantidae), 89–90
    hoofed animals (Ungulates), 87–88
    meat-eating predators (Carnivora), 96–102
    rodents (Rodentia), 77–79
    shrews and hedgehogs (Eulipotyphla), 81–83
    sloths and anteaters (Pilosa), 83–86
Marshall, S.L.A., 154
Mata Mata Turtle (Chelus fimbriata), 35–36
Maynard Smith, John, 117–119
Mayo clinic, 17
Middle management, 133
Mimicry, 141
Misery loves company, 109
monster.com, 187
Motion dazzle, 149
Muller, Fritz, 143
Mullerian mimicry, 143
Murphy's Law, 162
Mutualism, 104

N/Z-shaped ambush, 169–170
Nakajima, Sadahiko, 122
Narcissistic personality disorder, 14, 17–18
Nash equilibrium, 113, 115, 196
Nash, John, 111
National Health Service's (NHS), 14

Natural reluctance to kill, 154–158
Nature's clean-up crew, 50
Near ambush, 165
Neo-Luddites, 36
NHS. *See* National Health Service's
Nietzsche, Friedrich, 140
Nights out, 109

Obsessive-compulsive disorder
  (OCD), 83
OCD. *See* Obsessive-compulsive
  disorder
O-C-E-A-N, personality traits, 21
Ocelot, 43–44
Offensive strategies and tactics, 179
Offensive tactics, 176–
  booby traps, 176
  corporate sabotage, 176
  corporate terrorism, 177
Office territorialism, 107
Okapi (*Okapia johnstoni*), 87–88
Operational tactics, 154
Opportunity ambush, 163–164
Ordinal ranking, 116
Oregon State University, 128
*The Origin of the Species*, 2
Out of hours, 109
Out-of-work socializing, 110
Organizations, counterinsurgency
    techniques for
  propaganda, 206
    local elections and installment of
      new government, 207
    set up base and logistical hub for
      operations, 206–207
    support new government, 208
    wipe out insurgents, 207
    withdrawal, 208
  seven golden rules, 202
    guide, 203
    interpreter, 203–204
    leader, 204
    locate the guerrillas, 204–206
    logistical and equipment
      specialist, 204
    medic, 204
    set up a team of
      counterinsurgents, 203

Paenungulates, 89
Peregrine falcon (*Falco Peregrinus*), 47
Personality, 21–22
Phone call, 108, 150
Piranha (Serrasalmidae), 75–77
Playing dead, 158
Poincare, Henri, 102
Point ambush, 165
Prebattle considerations, 159–160
*Principles of Population*, 1
*The Prince*, 16
Prisoner's dilemma, 114–116
Prolonged hesitancy, 139
Psychological deflection, 140
Psychopath, 14
Pyrrhic victory, 159

Rainforest layers, 5–11
  security layer, 7–8
  service layer, 8–9
  specialist layer, 9–11
  strategic layer, 8
Rays (Batoidea), 73–75
Reaction formation, 128
Reconnaissance, 161–162
Reconnaissance, infiltration, and
    espionage, 160–162
Red-bellied piranhas (*Pygocentrus
    nattereri*), 76
Repression, 127
Reptiles, 29–39
  crocodiles, alligators, and caimans
    (crocodilians), 36–39
  snakes and lizards (squamites),
    30–34
  turtles and tortoises (testudines),
    34–36
Respect, 131–132
Rivalries and vendettas, 186
Rottweiler, 157

Sadness, 184–186
Scouting and patrolling, 162
Selfish herd theory, 198
Sharks (Selachimorpha), 71–73
Siamang (*Symphalangus syndactylus*),
    93
Skills, animal, 7

Skirmishes, 175–176
Social dilemma, 116–117
Sociopath, 14
South American rattlesnake (Crotalus durissus), 31
Spotlighting, 180–181
Stockholm syndrome, 127–128
Strategic deterrents, 153–154
Strategies, 181
Stress, 128–130
Success and enemies, 130–131
Sumatran tigers (Panthera tigris sondaica), 96–98
Sun, Tzu, 13, 135, 138, 141, 198
Superego, 20–21
Surrendering, 140–140
Systematic desensitization, 126

Takemoto-chock, Naomi, 21
Teamwork and loyalty, ants, 57
Thayer, Abbott Handerson, 148
The Art of War, 13, 135, 138, 141, 198
The central chimpanzee/tschego (Pan troglodytes troglodytes), 92
Thomson's caecilian (Caecilia Thompsoni), 29
Thor's hero shrew (Scutisorex thori), 82
Tonic immobility, shark, 73
Tracking, 162
Trapping, 151–152
Trust your instinct, 125
T-shaped ambush, 167
Tung, Mao Tse, 138
2019–2020 APPA (American Pet Products Association) National Pet Owners', 122
Two-way street, 131

U.S. Department of Defense's Pharmacoeconomic Center, 155
U.S. General Accounting Office (GAO), 153
U.S. General Ricardo Sanchez, 151–12
U.S. military, 153, 180
Unconsciously inept managers, 192

University of Herefordshire, 121
Unnatural selection, 104–112
   game theory, 111–112
Unorthodox method, 38
Urban warfare, 205

Vietnam War, 154
Vogelkop superb bird-of-paradise (Lophorina niedda), 43
von Neumann, John, 111
V-shaped ambush, 170–171
Vultures, 49–51

Warfare
   ambush strategy, 163–164
   ambush tactics, 164–168
   ambush, psychology of, 197–198
   baiting, 144–146
   bully, identifying and dealing, 187–189
   bullying, 187
   camouflage, 146
      background color matching, 146–147
      countershading, 148
      disruptive coloration, 147–148
      motion dazzle, 149
      self-decoration, 149
   collateral damage, 178
   corporate psychological warfare, 136
   deception, 141–144
   deflect, 140
   freeze, 138–140
   retreat, 137
   surrender, 140–141
   defending coworkers, 190
   effective counterinsurgency methods, 168–175
   engaging hr, benefits and limitations of, 189–190
   factors of influence, 198
   false flags, 179
   false movements and decoys, 151
   false retreats, 151
   gaslighting, 152–153
   hierarchies, 191–195
   human emotions, 181–186

Warfare (*contd.*)
  infrasound and ultrasound, 150
  natural reluctance to kill,
      154–158
  offensive strategies and tactics, 179
  offensive tactics, 176–
    booby traps, 176
    corporate sabotage, 176
    corporate terrorism, 177
  operational tactics, 154
  prebattle considerations, 159–160
  reconnaissance, infiltration, and
      espionage, 160–162
  rivalries and vendettas, 186
  skirmishes, 175–176
  strategic deterrents, 153–154
  strategies, 181
  trapping, 151–152
  winning by not winning, 195–196
Water-dwelling creatures,
      salamanders, 24
WhatsApp, 110
Wild jungle, 11
Winning by not winning, 195–196
Wiseman, Richard, 121
Wolf, Joseph, 126
"Wolf in sheep's clothing"
      approach, 141
World War II, 154

X-shaped ambush, 173

Zedong, Mao, 151
"Zero sum" games, 113

# OTHER TITLES IN OUR BUSINESS LAW AND CORPORATE RISK MANAGEMENT COLLECTION

John Wood, Econautics Sustainability Institute, *Editor*

- *Artificial Intelligence Design and Solution for Risk and Security* by Archie Addo
- *Artificial Intelligence for Security* by Archie Addo
- *Artificial Intelligence for Risk Management* by Archie Addo
- *The Business-Minded CISCO: How to Organize, Evangelize, and Operate an Enterprise-wide IT Risk Management Program* by Bryan C. Kissinger
- *Equipment Leasing and Financing: A Product Sales and Business Profit Center Strategy* by Richard M. Contino
- *Getting the Best Equipment Lease Deal: An Equipment Leasing Guide for Lessees* by Richard M. Contino
- *AI Concepts for Business Applications* by Nelson E. Brestoff
- *How New Risk Management Helps Leaders Master Uncertainty* by Robert B. Pojasek
- *Understanding Cyberrisks in IoT: When Smart Things Turn Against You* by Carolina A. Adaros Boye
- *The Business of Cybersecurity: Foundations and Ideologies* by Ashwini Sathnur
- *Cybersecurity Law: Protect Yourself and Your Customers* by Shimon Brathwaite
- *Conversations in Cyberspace* by Giulio D'Agostino
- *Board-Seeker: Your Guidebook and Career Map into the Corporate Boardroom* by Ralph Ward
- *Contract Law: A Comparison of Civil Law and Common Law Jurisdictions* by Claire-Michelle Smyth

## Concise and Applied Business Books

The Collection listed above is one of 30 business subject collections that Business Expert Press has grown to make BEP a premiere publisher of print and digital books. Our concise and applied books are for...

- Professionals and Practitioners
- Faculty who adopt our books for courses
- Librarians who know that BEP's Digital Libraries are a unique way to offer students ebooks to download, not restricted with any digital rights management
- Executive Training Course Leaders
- Business Seminar Organizers

**Business Expert Press** books are for anyone who needs to dig deeper on business ideas, goals, and solutions to everyday problems. Whether one print book, one ebook, or buying a digital library of 110 ebooks, we remain the affordable and smart way to be business smart. For more information, please visit **www.businessexpertpress.com**, or contact **sales@businessexpertpress.com**.

www.ingramcontent.com/pod-product-compliance
Lightning Source LLC
Chambersburg PA
CBHW061153220326
41599CB00025B/4471